Evangelization *for the* Third Millennium

by
Avery Cardinal Dulles, SJ

Paulist Press
New York/Mahwah, NJ

The Scripture quotations contained herein are from the author's own translation. Used by permission.

Cover design by Joy Taylor
Book design by Lynn Else

Copyright © 2009 by New York Province of the Society of Jesus

All rights reserved. No part of this book may be reproduced or transmitted in any form or by any means, electronic or mechanical, including photocopying, recording, or by any information storage and retrieval system without permission in writing from the Publisher.

Library of Congress Cataloging-in-Publication Data

Dulles, Avery, 1918–2008.
    Evangelization for the third millennium / by Avery Dulles.
        p. cm.
    ISBN 978-0-8091-4622-2 (alk. paper)
    1. Catholic Church—Missions. 2. Evangelistic work—Catholic Church. I. Title.
    BV2183.D85 2009
    266'.2—dc22

                                                                2009003494

Published by Paulist Press
997 Macarthur Boulevard
Mahwah, New Jersey 07430

www.paulistpress.com

Printed and bound in the
United States of America

Contents

Preface v

Abbreviations vii

1. Evangelization: New Testament through
   Vatican II 1

2. Paul VI and Evangelization 14

3. The Program: Paul VI, John Paul II, and the
   New Evangelization 30

4. The Gospel: Point of Contention and
   Convergence 42

5. Evangelization and Ecumenism 53

6. The Evangelization of Culture and the Catholic
   University 64

7. The New Evangelization and Theological
   Renewal 78

8. Models of Evangelization...90

9. Models of Catechesis 101

10. Models of Apologetics 115

Sources 128

Preface

Cardinal Dulles's appreciation of the significance of *Evangelii nuntiandi* (1975) deepened during his years as the Laurence J. McGinley Professor at Fordham University. During the last twenty years, Cardinal Dulles delivered twenty-three lectures, both here and abroad, pertaining to some aspect of evangelization. He also published eighteen articles on the topic; some of these articles were translated into other languages. Cardinal Dulles had long been planning to write a book on evangelization, but his busy schedule of lecturing, teaching, and writing commitments delayed his opportunity to do so. When a fall necessitated his moving to Murray-Weigel Hall, the Jesuit infirmary, in February 2007, he seriously began his work on this project, so dear to his heart.

Cardinal Dulles labored over the details of preparing this manuscript. Despite his rapidly declining health, he wanted to be involved in it, every step along the way. Michael M. Canaris, PhD candidate, the cardinal's graduate assistant, gathered the lectures and articles, and Cardinal Dulles chose the ten writings that appear in this book.

At first, he was able to edit the texts himself on his computer in the infirmary. After I prepared the manuscript, Cardinal Dulles read it and wrote his changes in the margins. But soon after making these corrections, he was no longer able to write, type, or speak. He read the next version of the manuscript and indicated further corrections by crumpling the bottom right-hand side of the page. When I went over the text, I would look for those pages that weren't smooth and then looked for the passage to be changed.

Although Paul VI is usually remembered for his encyclicals *Ecclesiam suam* (1964) and *Humanae vitae* (1968), Cardinal Dulles maintained that the pope's apostolic exhortation on evangelization was one of his greatest and most important contributions to the life of the Church in our time. It was the cardinal's hope that the present book would play a role in revitalizing this subject, and for this reason he devoted the last days of his life to working on it.

Cardinal Dulles was grateful for the help of our office staff throughout the publication process. I would like to add my gratitude to Mike Canaris, the cardinal's graduate assistant; Mrs. Maureen Noone, the cardinal's secretary, and Katelyn Moore and Stephany Rendón, our student workers—all of whom assisted me in completing the last book the cardinal wrote during his long and illustrious career of service to the Church.

As he now contemplates the vision of the God toward whom all evangelization tends, may Cardinal Dulles intercede for those of us who continue his work.

And may he enjoy hearing the words of his beloved Master, *"Well done, good and faithful servant."*

Anne-Marie Kirmse, OP, PhD
Assistant to Avery Cardinal Dulles, SJ
Fordham University
February 11, 2009
Feast of Our Lady of Lourdes

List of Abbreviations

AA   *Apostolicam actuositatem.* Vatican II's *Decree on the Apostolate of the Laity*

AG   *Ad gentes.* Vatican II's *Decree on the Church's Missionary Activity*

CA   *Centesimus annus.* Encyclical, John Paul II

CCC   *Catechism of the Catholic Church*

CD   *Christus Dominus.* Vatican II's *Decree on the Bishops' Pastoral Office in the Church*

CL   *Christifideles laici.* Apostolic exhortation, John Paul II

DCE   *Deus caritas est.* Encyclical, Benedict XVI

DH   *Dignitatis humanae.* Vatican II's *Declaration on Religious Freedom*

DS   Denzinger-Schönmetzer *Enchiridion Symbolorum*

DV   *Dei Verbum.* Vatican II's *Dogmatic Constitution on Divine Revelation*

EA   *Ecclesia in America.* Apostolic Exhortation, John Paul II

EE   *Ecclesia de Eucharistia.* Encyclical, John Paul II

EN   *Evangelii nuntiandi.* Apostolic exhortation, Paul VI

ES   *Ecclesiam suam.* Encyclical, Paul VI

FC   *Familiaris consortio.* Apostolic exhortation, John Paul II

FR   *Fides et ratio.* Encyclical, John Paul II

GS   *Gaudium et spes.* Vatican II's *Pastoral Constitution on the Church in the Modern World*

HV   *Humanae Vitae.* Encyclical, Paul VI

IM   *Inter mirifica.* Vatican II's *Decree on the Instruments of Social Communication*

JW   *Justice in the World.* 1971 Synod of Bishops

LG   *Lumen gentium.* Vatican II's *Dogmatic Constitution on the Church*

NA   *Nostra aetate.* Vatican II's *Declaration on the Relationship of the Church to Non-Christian Religions*

NMI   *Novo millennio ineunte.* Apostolic letter, John Paul II

OE   *Orientalium Ecclesiarum.* Vatican II's *Decree on Eastern Catholic Churches*

ORE   *L'Osservatore Romano.* Vatican newspaper, weekly English edition

PC   *Perfectae caritatis.* Vatican II's *Decree on the Appropriate Renewal of the Religious Life*

PO   *Presbyterorum ordinis.* Vatican II's *Decree on the Ministry and Life of Priests*

RH   *Redemptor hominis.* Encyclical, John Paul II

RMis   *Redemptoris missio.* Encyclical, John Paul II

SRS   *Sollicitudo rei socialis.* Encyclical, John Paul II

ST   *Summa theologica.* St. Thomas Aquinas

UR   *Unitatis redintegratio.* Vatican II's *Decree on Ecumenism*

UUS   *Ut unum sint.* Encyclical, John Paul II

VC   *Vita consecrata.* Apostolic exhortation, John Paul II

Chapter 1

Evangelization:
New Testament through
Vatican II

The term *evangelization* is biblical and goes back to the Old Testament. In the Greek Bible, the verb *evangelize* (*euaggelizesthai*) means to proclaim good news. In the Septuagint, the term occurs in the historical books, in the Psalms, and most prominently in Deutero-Isaiah. This last work has a famous description of the herald who runs ahead of the people on their return from Babylon to Jerusalem, proclaiming that Yahweh is triumphing over all his enemies and establishing his kingdom (Isa 52:7).

In the New Testament, the verb *euaggelizesthai* frequently appears in Luke, Acts, and the Pauline corpus. Jesus is anointed to proclaim the kingdom of God and evangelize the poor (Luke 4:18 and 7:22). After the Ascension, the apostles have the task of "preaching [*euaggelizomenoi*] Jesus Christ" (Acts 5:42). Quoting the previously mentioned passage in Deutero-Isaiah, Paul in Romans 10:15 exclaims: "How beautiful are the feet of those who bring [the] good news!" Paul is driven by a sense of his own call to be the Apostle to the Gentiles (Rom 15:20; 2 Cor 10:16; Gal 1:16; 2:7). Conscious of standing under a divine constraint, he exclaims, "Woe to me if I do not evangelize!" (1 Cor 9:16).

In the New Testament, therefore, the verb *evangelize* means to proclaim with authority and power the good news of salvation in Jesus Christ. The evangelist is one sent by Christ and endowed with a corresponding charism from the Holy Spirit. The preached word comes from God and arouses saving faith in those who believe it.

1

The Catholic Church has been involved in evangelization throughout its long history. In the early Middle Ages, monks such as Boniface in the West and Cyril in the East, with a veritable army of collaborators and followers, successfully evangelized almost the whole of Europe, erecting monasteries, cathedrals, churches, schools, and hospitals. After the great voyages of discovery in the fifteenth century, Catholic missionaries fanned out to spread the faith to North and South America, Africa, and Asia.

The crisis of evangelization has its roots in the Counter-Reformation, when the terms *gospel* and *evangelical* were taken over by Protestants and became suspect to Catholic ears. Catholics put the accent not so much on announcement as on teaching, not so much on the message of salvation as on the moral law, the Church, and the sacraments. Their missionary activity was therefore less evangelical and more ecclesiastical.

Responding to the Protestant Reformers, the Council of Trent at some points sounded a surprisingly evangelical note. In its discussion of the authorities to be used for teaching and conduct, the Council declared that the gospel was the source of all saving truth and moral discipline, and was to be preached to every creature (*DS* 1501). By this emphasis on the gospel and evangelization, the Catholic Church could have claimed to be in its own way evangelical.

In the next few centuries, however, Catholics shied away from speaking about the gospel and evangelization, since Protestant churches had appropriated these terms. The Catholic Church was content to be known as the Church of tradition, law, priesthood, and sacraments rather than the Church of the word of God.

In the modern period, moreover, the Catholic Church became preoccupied with the problems of schism and heresy. Great pains were taken to protect the faithful against modern errors. The Church as a whole turned in upon herself; she became more preoccupied with the instruction and pastoral care of her own members than with reaching out to new audiences. Missionary activity still went on, but it was seen as the preserve of apostolic religious orders and societies rather than a concern of the Church as a whole. The Catholic revival of the nineteenth century witnessed the foundation of many missionary orders and congregations, which still continue their labors.

The terminology of evangelization reentered Catholic literature toward the middle of the present century, thanks in part to the influence of Protestant thinkers such as Karl Barth. From the 1930s through the 1950s, Catholic religious educators promoted a new style of kerygmatic theology in which evangelization was taken to mean a confident proclamation of the basic message of God's offer of salvation through Jesus Christ. The kerygmatic sermons of Peter and Paul, as found in the Book of Acts, were studied as models for revitalizing the faith in dechristianized sections of Europe.

The future Pope John XXIII was exposed to the new kerygmatic theology during his years as nuncio to France, where he seems to have picked up many of his ideas for the Second Vatican Council. In the apostolic constitution *Humanae salutis* (1961), officially convoking the Council, he expressed his hope that the Council would "bring the modern world into contact with the vivifying and perennial energies of the gospel."[1] He called on the Council to demonstrate that the Church, "always living and always young, which feels the rhythm of the times and which in every century beautifies herself with new splendor, radiates new light, achieves new conquests...."[2] In his opening speech at the Council John XXIII expressed the hope that the Church would be able to draw all men and women of good will to herself not by threats and condemnations but by beneficence and gentle persuasion.[3]

Following these directives, Vatican II did in fact make evangelization one of its central themes, but this shift was scarcely noticed by the early commentators, most of whom interpreted the work of the Council in traditional Catholic categories. Vatican II became known for what it had said about the distribution of power in the Church, the reform of the liturgy, ecumenism, interfaith relations, and dialogue with the modern world—all themes of little or no interest to evangelicals.

In a document issued in 1975, Paul VI gave a radically different interpretation, emphasizing proclamation and the gospel. The objectives of the Council, he wrote, "are definitively summed up in this single one: to make the Church of the twentieth century ever better fitted for proclaiming the gospel to the people of the twentieth century" (*Evangelii nuntiandi* 2; hereafter *EN*). In this apostolic exhortation, Pope Paul fulfilled a request of the 1974 Assembly of the Synod of Bishops, which asked him to gather up the fruits of its labors, giving "a fresh forward impulse" and inaugurating what he called "a new period of evangelization" (ibid.). Rereading the Council documents in light of this statement, we can find considerable support for the pope's position.

The two great constitutions of Vatican II, those on the Church and on revelation, open on a strongly evangelical note. *Lumen gentium*, the *Dogmatic Constitution on the Church*, begins with the assertion that Christ is the light of all nations, and that the Church as his sacrament strives to shed on all human beings the radiance of Christ, which brightens her countenance as she proclaims the gospel to every creature (*LG* 1). *Dei Verbum*, the *Dogmatic Constitution on Divine Revelation*, begins with a strikingly kerygmatic passage. The Church, it affirms, "hearing the word of God with reverence and proclaiming it confidently," wishes to hand on Christ's message "so that by hearing the message of salvation the whole world may believe; by believing, it may hope; and by hoping, it may love" (*DV* 1).

The missionary spirit expressed in these passages permeates nearly all the documents of Vatican II. It is most evident, of course, in the splendid but rather neglected decree, *Ad gentes, Decree on the Church's Missionary Activity*. But the same spirit is evident in the *Decree on the Apostolate of the Laity*, which expounds at some length the ways in which lay men and women can suffuse the temporal sphere with the light and energy of the gospel, bearing witness to Christ by their words and their conduct. Passages in the Council documents that deal with bishops, priests, and liturgy emphasize the proclamatory dimension of the sacred ministry and the sacraments, especially that of the Eucharist, which is described as "the source and apex of the whole work of preaching the gospel" (*PO* 5). *The Pastoral Constitution on the Church in the Modern World, Gaudium et spes*, while speaking extensively of dialogue, gives equal attention to proclamation as a means of making the light of the gospel shine everywhere, fostering freedom and charity and transforming the human race into the family of God (*GS* 32, 41, 92).

In order to make these observations more concrete we may pose a series of questions about evangelization: its nature, its purposes, its bearers, its addressees, and its methods. All of these questions can, I believe, be adequately answered from documents of Vatican II.

What Is Evangelization?

The word *evangelization* originally meant the proclamation of the good news that the day of redemption had arrived. The gospel (*evangelion, evangelium*) is the good news, the saving message, heralded by an "evangelist." On many occasions, the Council cites the words of Paul to the Romans: "The gospel is the power of salvation to those who believe" (*UR* 21; cf. *LG* 19, 26; *DV* 17; *DH* 11). In the course of the centuries, the term *gospel* was increasingly objectified, so that it came to stand for the entire content of revelation. Vatican II sometimes uses the term to signify the basic message to be proclaimed, but sometimes more broadly, meaning the fullness of revelation given in Jesus Christ. Unlike Lutherans, Catholics do not divide revelation into law and gospel. God's revealed law is part of the gospel.

Evangelization, accordingly, has two senses. In the narrow sense, it means the announcement of the global Christian message to those who do not believe, that is to say, primary evangelization. But in a broad sense it means everything that brings human life and the world under the sway of God's word. In this second sense, evangelization practically coincides with the total mission of the Church. Normally, if not in every case, Vatican II used the term *evangelization* in the narrow sense, to mean the action of announcing Christ rather than of bringing his influence to bear upon diverse persons and situations through education, pastoral care, and social action.

Why Evangelize?

Christians, who confess Christ to be the Savior of the world, should have no difficulty in finding motives for evangelization in any of the forms just mentioned. Vatican II frequently quotes the final charge of the risen Christ to the apostles: to preach the gospel to all the nations of the world. This missionary mandate, as expressed in Mark 16:15, is quoted or referenced at least a dozen times (*LG* 1, 16, 19, and 24; *DV* 7; *UR* 2; *OE* 3; *AG* 1, 5, and 38; *PO* 4; and *DH* 13). Matthew 28:19–20, which reiterates the same mandate, is cited only slightly less frequently (e.g., *LG* 17, 19, and 24; *DV* 7; *AG* 5; *DH* 13 and 14). Obedience to the Lord's command is therefore the primary motive for evangelization.

Supplementing the argument from authority, the Council proposes intrinsic reasons for missionary activity: it contributes to the glory of God and the salvation of human beings. God is glorified when his saving work in Christ is acknowledged, when hymns of praise and thanksgiving rise to him, and when people shape their lives according to his teaching. In turning to Christ, men and women benefit themselves. Christ delivers them from the power of sin. As they receive the gifts of grace, they are made sharers in God's inner trinitarian life (*LG* 17; *AG* 7–8).

The decree *Ad gentes* teaches that missionary activity is an intrinsic demand of the Church's own catholicity. Tending by her very nature to express her catholicity, she realizes herself by proclaiming God's word to the nations and thereby contributing to the establishment of God's kingdom everywhere (*AG* 1).

Vatican II is careful not to reject authentic values that exist in the world before it is touched by the gospel. Evangelization, it declares, preserves everything good that is to be found in human cultures or religions, frees it from admixture with evil, and elevates it to a higher plane. "Whatever good is in the minds and hearts of men, whatever good lies latent in the religious practices and cultures of diverse peoples, is not only saved from destruction but is also healed, ennobled, and perfected unto the glory of God, the confusion of the devil, and the happiness of man" (*LG* 17; cf. *GS* 58).

The Council did not fail to address the question of the necessity of the Church. She is indeed necessary because God has associated her inseparably with Christ as his Mystical Body. Having made her a universal sign of salvation, he uses her as his instrument for the redemption of all (*LG* 9). All who attain salvation, therefore, depend on the mediation of the Church as well as upon Christ the divine Mediator. Those who are in a position to recognize Christ as Savior are bound to believe and to confess him by joining the Church (*LG* 14).

To the question whether it is possible for people to be saved without actually hearing and accepting the good news of Jesus Christ, the Council answers with a qualified affirmative. If with the help of God's grace they do what they can to conform to God's will, God will make it possible for them to attain salvation in some way known to himself (*LG* 16; *AG* 7; *GS* 22). But if they hear and accept the gospel, they will have many additional helps to salvation: the guidance of revelation, the pastoral care of the Church, and the graces of the sacraments. Lacking these helps, people are often deceived into exchanging the truth of God for a lie (*LG* 16).

The comprehensive vision of the Council is splendidly displayed in *LG* 17, which states as follows:

> The Church is compelled by the Holy Spirit to do her part towards the full realization of the will of God, who has established Christ as the source of salvation for the whole world. By the proclamation of the gospel, she prepares her hearers to receive and profess the faith, disposes them for baptism, snatches them from the slavery of error, and incorporates them into Christ so that through charity they may grow into full maturity in Christ....
>
> In this way the Church simultaneously prays and labors in order that the entire world may become the People of God, the Body of the Lord, and the Temple of the Holy Spirit, and that in Christ, the Head of all, there may be rendered to the Creator and Father of the Universe all honor and glory.

Who Should Be Evangelized?

Vatican II many times states that all men and women are to be evangelized. It makes no exceptions because the rationale for evangelization applies to all, no matter what their race, nationality, gender, or social condition.

Since the Council, some theologians have suggested that Christians ought not to trouble adherents of other religions by proclaiming Christ to them. Since it is possible for such persons to be saved without becoming Christians, it is argued, we should leave them in good faith, helping them to live good lives in their own religious tradition. As a general policy, this practice would be unsound and contrary to the teaching of Vatican II. As a matter of pastoral prudence, however, it is sometimes advisable to wait for an opportune moment before confronting certain persons or groups with the claims of the gospel. They may need to be better prepared in order to hear it fruitfully.

Some contemporary Christians have maintained that there is no need to evangelize Jews, because Jews already enjoy a salvific covenant relationship with God. Having treated that question elsewhere,[4] I do not want to go through that whole discussion again, but for present purposes it may suffice to say that Vatican II makes no exception for Jews. It teaches simply that the gospel is to be proclaimed to every creature. Jesus Christ died for all and wills that all come to a knowledge of the truth. Believing Jews, of course, are not in the same condition as pagans. They already have the word of God as given in the Law and the prophets. But by acknowledging Jesus as the promised Messiah and Lord to whom their ancestors looked forward, Jews give additional glory to God and enter into the blessings of the new and perfect Covenant, prefigured by the old (*LG* 9).

The question could be raised whether Catholics should evangelize other Christians. According to the teaching of Vatican II, these others are not fully initiated into the Body of Christ. Baptism is only the first sacrament of initiation and demands to be completed by the Eucharist (*UR* 22). Full communion requires acceptance of the Church's entire system and admission to the Eucharist, the sacrament of full communion (*LG* 14). Since the whole creed and the dogmas of the Church, as well as the sacraments and pastoral government, pertain to the gospel, it follows logically that Christians who are not Catholics still require additional evangelization. But Vatican II, as I have mentioned, does not seem to use the term *evangelization* in this broader sense.

Missionary activity includes evangelization and the planting of the Church (*AG* 6), but it does not include the pastoral care of the faithful or undertakings aimed at the restoration of unity among Christians (ibid.; cf. *UR* 4). Having said that, the Council goes on to point out that both these activities are closely connected with missionary activity and consequently with evangelization. Pastoral care arouses zeal for evangelization in individuals and communities (*AG* 39). Division among Christians is a serious impediment to evangelization, since it blocks the way to faith for many. "Hence, by the same mandate which makes missions necessary, all the baptized are called to be gathered into one flock, and thus to be able to bear unanimous witness before the nations to Christ their Lord" (*AG* 6; cf. *UR* 1).

By the same token, it may be asked whether Catholics are still in need of evangelization. Many who have been baptized into the Catholic Church have not yet heard the gospel convincingly proclaimed. Some who have been catechized have never captured the basic Christian vision. They know many doctrines of the Church but seem never to have encountered the living Christ. They could certainly profit from hearing the kind of proclamation that is designed to bring nonbelievers to faith.

In passages dealing with evangelization, Vatican II did not speak to the question of unevangelized Catholics, except perhaps in one passage. In the *Decree on the Church's Missionary Activity*, the Council alluded in passing to the problem of dechristianization. It said that changes can occur in previously evangelized areas that call for a renewal of missionary activity (*AG* 6).

Even without using the term *evangelization* for ministry to marginal and inactive Catholics, the Council called attention to their need for a fresh encounter with the gospel. In Scripture reading, preaching, and Bible study, the faithful continually renew and energize their commitment. "The force and power of the word of God is so great that it remains the support and energy of the

Church, the strength of faith for her sons, the food of the soul, and the pure and perennial source of spiritual life" (*DV* 21).

Who Should Evangelize?

In recent centuries, Catholics have commonly looked upon evangelization as the task of persons who receive a special call to become preachers or missionaries. The main body of the faithful considered that their task was not to extend the faith but to receive God's grace and live according to the gospel. Vatican II made a new step forward. At many points it insisted that the whole Church is missionary and that every member is obliged to take part in disseminating the gospel. "The obligation of spreading the faith," it stated, "is imposed on every disciple of Christ, according to his ability" (*LG* 17; cf. *AA* 35). But the obligation, it recognized, does not rest upon all in the same way. People in different states of life have different obligations.

The Dogmatic Constitution on the Church opens its discussion of the episcopal office with the words: "Among the principal duties of bishops, the preaching of the gospel occupies an eminent place. For bishops are preachers of the faith who lead new disciples to Christ" (*LG* 25). The diocesan bishop, it states, must be "ready to preach the gospel to all (cf. Rom 1:14–15) and to urge his faithful to apostolic and missionary activity" (*LG* 27). The *Decree on the Church's Missionary Activity* teaches that "the responsibility to proclaim the gospel throughout the world falls primarily on the body of bishops" (*AG* 29). Missionary activity is "a supremely great and sacred task of the Church" (ibid.). Both individually in their dioceses and in councils and conferences, bishops are required to stimulate, organize, and direct evangelization.

Diocesan priests carry on the work of ministry in parishes, extending and applying the ministry of the bishop. In their pastoral activity, they are exhorted to "stir up and preserve among the faithful a zeal for the evangelization of the world" (*AG* 39). Both the *Decree on the Religious Life* and the *Decree on the Church's Missionary Activity* mention the prominent role traditionally played by religious orders, both active and contemplative, in missionary evangelization (*PC* 20; *AG* 18; cf. *LG* 44).

"The laity," says *Lumen gentium*, "are called in a special way to make the Church present and operative in those places and circumstances where only through them can she become the salt of the earth" (*LG* 33). "This evangelization," it adds, "that is, this announcing of Christ by a living testimony as well as by the spoken word, takes on a specific quality and a special force in that it is carried out in the ordinary surroundings of the world" (*LG* 35). The Christian family can be an outstanding example of testimony to Christ and the gospel (ibid.).

Other documents, such as the *Decree on the Apostolate of the Laity*, strongly emphasize the involvement of the laity in the evangelization of the settings in which they live and work. The Council also encouraged the laity to cooperate in ministries designed to build up the Church herself. Some lay persons, it noted, receive a special vocation to work with the hierarchy in teaching Christian doctrine, in liturgical services, and in the care of souls (*AA* 24). Organizations such as Catholic Action exemplify the collaboration of lay persons in the apostolate proper to the hierarchy (*AA* 20).

Ways of Evangelization

Among the many paths of evangelization, the most obvious is the preaching of the gospel, which the *Decree on the Church's Missionary Activity* describes as the "chief means" of implanting the Church (*AG* 6). But when circumstances prevent the direct and immediate announcement of the gospel, Christians can bear witness to Christ very effectively by charity and works of mercy (ibid.). The laity, in particular, can exercise a fruitful apostolate by their conduct in the areas of their labor, profession, studies, neighborhood, and social life. And according to the *Decree on the Apostolate of the Laity*, they will look for opportunities to announce Christ to their neighbors through the spoken word as well (*AA* 13).

Proclamation of the gospel should always take account of particular cultural contexts. Without using the term *inculturation*, *Gaudium et spes* conveyed the idea. "This accommodated preaching of the gospel," it declared, "ought to remain the law of all evangelization" (*GS* 44). The gospel has a transformative impact on the cultures it encounters. "By the very fulfillment of her mission," says the Council, "the Church stimulates and advances human and civic culture" (*GS* 58). The gospel "strengthens, perfects, and renews them [cultures] in Christ" (ibid.; cf. *GS* 61). Popes Paul VI and John Paul II would have a great deal more to say about the evangelization of cultures.

Evangelization can also take the form of social action, even though the proper and proximate goal of such activity is innerworldly and natural. By promoting right order of values in their earthly activities, Christians practice faithfulness to the gospel and win respect for it. Allowing their whole lives to be permeated by the spirit of the beatitudes, they promote justice and charity in society (*GS* 72).

Vatican II at a number of points disavowed what it called unworthy methods of evangelization. No one should seek to gain converts by appealing to merely temporal motives, by offering false promises, by physical or psychological coercion, or by falsely demeaning other churches or religions. According to the *Declaration on Religious Freedom*, the adherence of faith must always be physically and psychologically free (*DH* 2, 4, 10; *AG* 13).

St. Paul quotes the Psalmist as saying, "I believed, and so I spoke" (2 Cor 4:13; cf. Ps 116:10). Belief, where it is healthy and strong, naturally expresses itself in words and actions. If Catholics do not evangelize, the fundamental obstacle does not lie so much in the surrounding culture as in themselves. Having failed to nourish their faith by study, prayer, and contemplation, many have become weak and flabby in their adherence to the gospel and the Church. If they personally grasped the vision of faith, they would joyfully give witness to Christ, even at the cost of wealth, honors, and life itself. Perhaps their faith is weak because they have not tried to share it. As John Paul II wisely observed, "faith is strengthened when it is given to others" (*RMis* 2). Vatican II called upon every Christian, whether bishop, priest, religious, or lay, to evangelize by word, by personal example, and by helping to transform society according to the mind of Christ. An increasing group of young Catholics, I believe, are sensing the urgency of this project.

Notes

1. John XXIII, "Apostolic Constitution *Humanae salutis*," *The Documents of Vatican II*, ed. Walter M. Abbott (New York: America Press, 1966), 703.

2. Ibid., 706.

3. John XXIII, Opening Speech at the Council, ibid., 710–19, esp. 716.

4. Avery Cardinal Dulles, "The Covenant with Israel," *First Things* 157 (November 2005): 16–21.

Chapter 2

Paul VI and Evangelization

Paul VI preeminently merits the title of an evangelizing pope. Succeeding John XXIII in 1963, he took the name of Paul in honor of the Apostle of the Gentiles. The first pope since 1809 to travel abroad, he made nine apostolic journeys: the Holy Land (1964), India (1964), New York City (1965), Portugal (1967), Turkey (1967), Colombia (1968), Geneva (1969), and the Far East (Teheran, East Pakistan, Philippines, West Samoa, Australia, Indonesia, Hong Kong, and Sri Lanka [1970]). Sensitive to the unpopularity of the colonial system, he spoke of the Church as being at home in all cultures, encouraged inculturation, and exhorted Africans to be missionaries to one another.

In his reorganization of the Roman Curia in 1967, Paul VI renamed the Congregation for the Propagation of the Faith, calling it the Congregation for the Evangelization of Peoples, thus softening the distinction between missionary activity (to places where the gospel had not yet taken root) and evangelization (which could be carried on in areas already Christianized).

Paul VI chose as the theme for the 1974 assembly of the Synod of Bishops "the evangelization of the modern world." On the basis of materials submitted to him by the assembly, in 1975 he composed his great postsynodal apostolic exhortation, *Evangelii nuntiandi* (*EN*), commemorating the tenth anniversary of the close of Vatican II.

As noted in chapter 1, the commentaries on Vatican II published in the first decade after the Council (1965–75) generally overlooked the centrality of evangelization. They focused attention on collegiality, ecumenism, dialogue, and social teaching. But Paul VI, who had played a major part in shaping the agenda of the Council even before his election to the papacy, corrected this oversight. In *Evangelii nuntiandi*, he declared that the objectives of the Second Vatican Council could be definitively summed up under a single heading: "...to make the Church of the twentieth century ever better fitted for proclaiming the gospel to the people of the twentieth century" (*EN* 2). In this document Paul VI expressed his hope of giving a "fresh forward impulse" and launching what he called "a new period of evangelization" (ibid.).[1] In some fifty pages he presented for the first time in history a magisterial treatment of the nature, aims, and methods of evangelization, the contents of which will be described in future chapters. To indicate the context in which Pope Paul was writing, it may be of interest to survey some early reactions.

Delayed Response

When it was first published, *EN* did not make the impact that might have been expected. Commentators later suggested that it came at a bad time, just before the Christmas rush,[2] and that it disappeared behind the clouds of dust raised by controversies about sexual morality after the issuance of the declaration *Persona humana* by the Congregation for the Doctrine of the Faith.[3] In the United States, the launching of the bicentennial festivities was an additional distraction.[4]

After about six months some serious studies did begin to appear in various languages. On the ground that *EN* had not yet received due attention, the *Neue Zeitschrift für Missionswissenschaft*, a Swiss review, published a theme issue on *EN* late in 1976.[5] The most voluminous commentary, some nine hundred pages in length, came out in Rome, from the Pontificia Università Urbaniana in 1977. José Saraiva Martins, in his introduction, remarked that after two years no full organic commentary had appeared—a fact he attributed to the prevalence of opinions at variance with the pope's teaching.[6]

Some of the early articles contented themselves with expounding the contents of the pope's exhortation, almost without evaluative comment.[7] Others attempted to categorize the document. It was variously described as a "true treatise on evangelization,"[8] as a personal "meditation" or "colloquium,"[9] and as an invitation for the reader to meditate with the pope.[10] Without denying its personal and meditative character, one author pointed out that in *EN* the pope accomplished what the Synod left unfinished, "namely, to piece together a sufficiently systematic theological description of the Church's evangelizing mission."[11]

Several authors commented that the pope's purpose was to seek reconciliation among different schools of thought rather than to achieve sharp definitions.[12] One English writer pointed out the rather remarkable common ground between the pope's exhortation and the report of section 1 of the Nairobi Assembly of the World Council of Churches on "Confessing the Faith Today."[13]

Favorable Reactions

Laudatory comments were not lacking. *EN* was characterized as "one of the essential texts of the pontificate of Paul VI," one that "merits profound study."[14] Another author called it a "magisterial exposition that summarizes for our time the doctrinal and methodological insights of the present-day Church," takes cognizance of the signs of our time on the ways of mission, and is "able to arouse a new impulse, capable of creating within the Church a new age of evangelization."[15] Still another praised it for being "the first papal pronouncement to explain organically, in the doctrinal perspective of Vatican II, the true nature, dynamism, and saving efficacy of the gospel message, and to indicate to the Church new methods of evangelization for our difficult times."[16] *EN*, said another commentator, "touched upon all the problems that endanger evangelization in the modern world."[17] An Irish theologian noted that, in spite of disappointing sections, it was one of the most hopeful and inspiring documents issued in recent years.[18]

In a North American conference marking the tenth anniversary of *EN*, Eugene LaVerdiere, a specialist on New Testament exegesis and missiology, wrote that it was "widely recognized as the greatest and most far-reaching Church document issued since Vatican II," and that, if taken seriously, it could "bring about the transformation of the Church inaugurated by the council."[19] The

Paulist Alvin A. Illig declared: "The course for the rest of this century has been set by Pope Paul, the modern evangelizer. We have the charter before us: *Evangelii nuntiandi*, 'The Gospels must be proclaimed.'"[20]

A number of authors observed that the manner of production of this apostolic exhortation furnished a model for the functioning of the magisterium of the universal Church.[21] Besides expressing the views of the pope himself, *EN* reflected ideas coming from the world's bishops' conferences, and at many points echoed the voice of the Synod of 1974, which had asked the pope to complete its own labors. "Those who followed the work [of the Synod]," wrote Philippe Delhaye, "find it easy to put names on certain paragraphs that summarize the interventions, for example, on the importance of the homily (no. 43), mass media (no. 45), secularism (no. 54), the action of the Holy Spirit (no. 75), popular religiosity in Latin America (no. 48), and the necessity of doctrinal firmness (no. 79)."[22]

Among the points singled out for special praise, mention must be made of its clarification of the meaning of the term *evangelization*. The *lineamenta* for the Synod on Evangelization had proposed four definitions, none of which was entirely satisfactory to the Synod itself. With the help of the Synod, Paul VI chose a very comprehensive concept, in which Bishop Saraiva finds three organically connected dimensions: the explicit proclamation of the gospel, the testimony of life, and the celebration of the sacraments.[23] To these three dimensions the pope, as others point out, added the formation of ecclesial community and the participation of that community in apostolic initiatives.[24] Still others mention that evangelization, as the pope described it, must effect a profound renewal in those who experience it.[25]

Favorable commentators spoke of the remarkable agreement between the exhortation and the biblical concept of evangelization.[26] According to one author, the pope's concept of testimony constituted a prophetic forward step in the theology of evangelization.[27] Others praised the clarification whereby catechesis was integrated into the broad concept of evangelization rather than being allowed to stand simply outside it.[28] Several years later in the United States, a specialist on catechetics, synthesizing *EN* with John Paul's apostolic exhortation *Catechesi tradendae*, showed at some length how the process of catechization enters into evangelization, for instance, in the Rite of Christian Initiation of Adults.[29]

Others noted the way in which liberation and human development were felicitously built into the pope's teaching on evangelization, without detriment to the primacy of word and testimony.[30] The pope was also praised for his tactful way of speaking of the non-Christian religions, so that they could serve as a basis of preevangelization, while at the same time taking account of the necessity of proclaiming the gospel to all peoples.[31] Regarding basic Christian communities, some authors considered that the pope had rendered an important service in formulating criteria for their ecclesial authenticity, separating the good grain from the chaff.[32] Several members of religious orders expressed appreciation of the pope's praise for the religious life as an actuation of consecration to God in radical form.[33]

A number of authors praised the pope for his carefully nuanced views on the relationships between evangelization and cultures. Hervé Carrier spoke of *EN* as "a true charter for the evangelization of cultures." Drawing inspiration from Vatican II, he said, the pope "greatly clarified its analysis, translating it into more practical lines of action."[34] Another author showed at length how the synergy between culture and evangelization, as interpreted in *EN*, points toward a qualitative leap in their mutual fructification.[35]

Still another merit found by some authors in *EN* was the ample space devoted to the role of the laity.[36] They are not reduced to mere auxiliaries, said one critic, but are assigned a specific role.[37] The mission of the laity is treated in a way that reflects the theologies of history and of secularization of the preceding thirty years.[38]

Critical Comments

It was not to be expected, however, that the reception would be uniformly enthusiastic, given the intention of *EN* to check several negative tendencies at work within the Catholic community. The editorial staff of Concilium devoted a special issue "to show in some detail how unconvincing the apostolic exhortation *Evangelii nuntiandi* of Pope Paul VI (1975) has proved to be."[39] One article in this issue said that in asking the pope to write up "single-handed" the conclusions of the Synod, the bishops had violated an "elementary principle of sound procedure." The same article lamented that the pope had fallen into dichotomies such as material vs. spiritual, temporal vs. eternal, immanent vs. transcendent, secular vs. religious, natural vs. revealed, and priests vs. people. "More egalitarian and less mystifying notions," said the authors of this article, would have been appropriate.[40]

Theologians wedded to the terminology of the "kerygmatic" school maintained that the pope, in his broad definition, overlooked the primary meaning of the term *evangelization*, namely the announcement of the good news to those who are afar.[41] The respective merits of Paul VI's broad definition and the missiologists' narrower concept of evangelization became a subject of debate.[42] Some religious educators objected that *EN* improperly blurred the distinction between evangelization and catechesis, rendering it difficult to discern the particular functions and laws of each.[43] In a similar way, another commentator protested that in saying that preevangelization "is already evangelization in a true sense," the pope had broadened the terms to the point where they meant next to nothing.[44] One missiologist expressed his regrets that Paul VI seemed to make too little use of the term *mission*, practically substituting for it his broad concept of *evangelization*.[45]

A significant group of critics complained that the pope's treatment of non-Christian religious was too negative. One Concilium author remarked that although the pope expressed respect for these religions, his acceptance of the Church's claim to universality "makes dialogue intrinsically impossible."[46] Without going to this extreme, others considered that the pope had been insufficiently positive in his treatment of other faiths. Jacques Dupuis, SJ, judges that *EN*'s evaluation of other religions seems unduly negative and that it leaves little room for interreligious dialogue.[47] Michael L. Fitzgerald, from a similar perspective, objects that the pope did not advert sufficiently to the work of the Holy Spirit in these religions and to the value of their popular piety. He concludes that in *EN* the theme of the religions is insufficiently developed and lacks precision, but he adds that of course *EN* is to be interpreted as an exhortation rather than a dogmatic statement or a pastoral directory.[48] Another missiologist, besides objecting to the classification of non-Christian religions as merely natural, finds it unfortunate that in *EN* 54 the pope seems to regard the members of other Christian churches as objects of mission.[49] Donal Dorr, for his part, remarks that the pope's portrayal of the non-Christian religions as searching for God gives the misleading impression that they do not find him.[50]

A further criticism that appears in the literature about *EN* is that it reflects the typical Roman preoccupations: the importance of universality, allergy to criticism from below, and hesitation regarding political involvement.[51] The tone of *EN*, some said, is worried and cautious, probably because the pope was alarmed by the brashness of the Third-World bishops' self-assertion.[52] Further specifying this reservation, various authors accused the pope of being unduly nervous about watering down of the gospel and Catholic doctrine,[53] and perhaps too hesitant about the value of theological pluralism.[54] Authors strongly committed to the growth of basic Christian communities regarded the pope's exhortation as being excessively defensive and mistrustful regarding these units.[55]

The pope's criticisms of Marxist socialism and his expressed opposition to the theology of revolution provoked some negative reactions. One of the Concilium authors, while praising the pope for his openness to reform, faulted him for his hostility to liberation theology and his failure to endorse conflict and revolution as models of socialization.[56] Donal Dorr wrote that the pope missed a great opportunity by condemning violence as a means of changing social structures but saying nothing about violence that supports unjust social structures.[57] The Spanish Jesuit Francisco Ivern took exception to *EN* for its vagueness about the relationship between evangelization and the promotion of justice in the world. What is meant, he asked, by the "profound links" between the two, mentioned in *EN* 31? Is it enough to say, with *EN* 30, that to assist in liberation from material distress is "not foreign to evangelization"? Did the pope intend to reaffirm, or to dilute, the assertion of the Synod of Bishops in 1971 to the effect that action on behalf of justice was a "constitutive dimension" of the preaching of the gospel?[58] After noting that the pope warns against instrumentalizing the gospel in the service of sociopolitical liberation, Ivern comments that the gospel can also be instrumentalized by people "who 'do theology' to defend and justify their interests and privileges, their inertia, their isolation from reality, and their lack of evangelical courage"[59]

An even stronger criticism is that of Paul Valladier, editor of *Études.* He describes *EN* as a nonhistorical approach that neglects the concrete challenges of politics, economics, and nationalism in different ecclesial situations. In the pope's treatment of the "ways of evangelization," he observes, only the verbal and religious aspects are mentioned, to the neglect of the social, political, and economic. In summary, he says, *EN* deals with the need of the world for the Church, but overlooks the need of the Church for the world. The papal document deals with only one aspect of the dialectic and one half of the problem.[60] The criticisms are not self-evidently valid. They depend upon certain options and priorities contrary to, or at least not identical with, those of Paul VI. In his effort to correct what he regarded as an excessive emphasis on the dialogic and the sociopolitical, the pope was deliberately emphasizing proclamation through word and personal testimony. He was opposing what may be called theological "crosscurrents," which would promote the local community at the expense of Catholic universalism, interreligious dialogue at the expense of proclamation, and social action at the expense of religious practice.[61]

Some defenders of *EN* went to the opposite extreme from the critics just mentioned. An article in *Communio,* after surveying many of the reactions to *EN,* concludes that the supporters as well as the critics show an interest in evangelization only because of its this-worldly effects in liberating the oppressed or transforming cultures. The author maintains that for Paul VI the primary motive for evangelization is to stir up faith and thus to bring individual believers to eternal salvation. The Southern Baptists and the Assemblies of God, he contends, experience significant growth because, unlike many Catholics of our day, they focus on personal, eternal salvation.[62]

Implementation

I cannot here report on the implementation of *EN* in the whole Western world. It may suffice to say that in United States *EN* has been enthusiastically welcomed by the bishops and by various national organizations as a basis for action. In 1977 the National Conference of Catholic Bishops set up an ad hoc Committee on Evangelization, which in November 1990 was to become a permanent standing committee and is today known as the Bishops' Committee on Evangelization (BCEV). In the early years, this committee was located in the Secretariat for the American Board of Catholic Missions. In 2000, however, the office was moved into the full-standing Secretariat for Evangelization.

Also in 1977 the Paulists established in Washington the headquarters of the Paulist Catholic Evangelization Association. Under the leadership of Rev. Alvin Illig, CSP, and his successor, Rev. Kenneth Boyack, CSP, this committee has been very active in promoting conferences and programs of evangelization for dioceses and parishes.

On November 18, 1992, the bishops of the United States, by an overwhelming vote of 229 to 2, adopted the document *Go and Make Disciples: A National Plan and Strategy for Catholic Evangelization in the United States.*[63] This document was republished in a tenth-anniversary edition in 2002 with a commemorative foreword by Francis Cardinal George. Part 1, "The Vision of Catholic Evangelization," is taken almost exclusively from *EN.* The bishops define *evangelization* as "bringing the good news of Jesus into every human situation and seeking to convert individuals and society by the divine power of the gospel itself. Its essence is the proclamation of salvation in Jesus Christ and the response of a person in faith, both being the work of the Spirit of God." Three goals for evangelization are set forth: to animate Catholics to share their faith, to invite all Americans to hear the message of salvation in Jesus Christ, and to foster gospel values in society. The bishops' strategy for implementation includes many detailed suggestions for the renewal of the parish and its liturgy, for individual and group retreats, for Bible study, for the witness of personal example in the home and the workplace, and for the building of warm and welcoming communities. Gradually, after many years, the vision of *EN* would seem to be leading to a measure of renewal at the level of parish and home life.

The United States bishops have not confined their interest to evangelization in their own country. In 1986 they issued a pastoral statement on world mission, *To the Ends of the Earth*, which made ample use of *Evangelii nuntiandi* as well as the documents of Vatican II.[64]

Many other initiatives by the BCEV may be noted. In 1998 it published the document *A Time to Listen, A Time to Heal: A Resource Directory for Reaching Out to Inactive Catholics*. In October 2000 it collaborated with the committees of Ecumenical and Interreligious Affairs, Education, Liturgy, and Pastoral Practices for the publication of *Journey to the Fullness of Life: A Report on the Implementation of the Rite of Christian Initiation of Adults in the United States*. It has sponsored biennial convocations for diocesan evangelization directors.

The BCEV established the US Commission on Catholic Evangelization with its three committees: Diocesan Evangelization Ministries, Intercultural Ministries, and National Catholic Organizations. The BCEV also sponsors the North American Institute for Catholic Evangelization (NAICE).

In assessing the reception of *EN*, one must add that John Paul II's proposals for a "new evangelization" are heavily indebted to the apostolic exhortation of his predecessor. In *Crossing the Threshold of Hope*, he declares that *EN*, although not issued in the form of an encyclical, "in its great importance...perhaps surpasses many encyclicals."[65] The response to *EN* is by now inextricably interwoven with the response to the program of John Paul II.

Notes

1. Paul VI did not actually use the term *new evangelization*, but it had already been used in 1968 by the Latin American bishops at Medellín in their "Message to the Peoples of Latin America." See General Conference of the Latin American Bishops,

The Church in the Present-Day Transformation of Latin America in the Light of the Council, II, *Conclusions* (Bogotá, Colombia: General Secretariat of CELAM, 1970), 41.

2. Richard L. Stewart, "Confessing Christ," *Clergy Review* 61 (1976): 422–29, at 422.

3. Jan Snijders, "*Evangelii Nuntiandi*: The Movement of Minds," *Clergy Review* 62 (1977): 170–75, at 170.

4. Frederick L. Miller, "*Evangelii Nuntiandi* and the Parish Priest," *Homiletic and Pastoral Review* 76 (June 1976): 46–57, at 46.

5. *Neue Zeitschrift für Missionswissenschaft* 32 (1976). See editor's note, 241.

6. José Saraiva Martins, "Introduzione," *L'Annuncio del Vangelo Oggi: Commento all'Esortazione Apostolica di Paolo VI, Evangelii Nuntiandi* (Rome: Pontificia Università Urbaniana, 1977), ix–xv, at xi.

7. E.g, Bede McGregor, "Commentary on *Evangelii Nuntiandi*," *Doctrine and Life* (Special Issue, March/April 1977): 53–97. Also Antonio di Monda, "Evangelizzazione dei popoli da parte della Chiesa nella Esortazione Apostolic Evangelii nuntiandi," *Palestra de clero* 55 (1976): 676–89, which contains some laudatory comments at the end of the summary. Similarly objective is Giuseppe de Rosa, "Significato e Contenuto di 'Evangelizzazione,'" *Civiltà cattolica*, no. 3040 (1977), 321–36. De Rosa does however give *EN* credit for probably signalizing the end-point of the semantic development of the term *evangelization* (330), and at the close of his article he raises some questions about the relationship between human advancement and evangelization.

8. Paul Valladier, "L'Évangélisation dans le monde moderne," *Études* 344 (January–June 1976): 605–10, at 606.

9. Snijders, "Movement of Minds," 170; cf. 175.

10. Donal Dorr, "*Evangelization in the Modern World*—Reflections on Pope Paul's Document," *Furrow* 27 (1976): 531–39, at 531. Eugene LaVerdiere characterizes it as "both a meditation and an invitation to meditation," in "A Scriptural Meditation on *Evangelii Nuntiandi*," in *Catholic Evangelization Today*, ed. Kenneth Boyack (New York: Paulist, 1987), 11–21, at 11.

11. David Bohr, *Evangelization in America* (New York: Paulist, 1977), 78.

12. E.g., Snijders, "Movement of Minds," 171. Paul Tihon speaks of the pope's concern to overcome controversies, "Des missions à la mission: la problématique missionnaire depuis Vatican II," *Nouvelle revue théologique* 107 (1985): 520–36, 698–721, at 704.

13. Stewart, "Confessing Christ," 423–29.

14. Philippe Delhaye, "L'Évangélisation chrétienne aujourd'hui: une relecture du Synode de 1974 par S.S. Paul VI," *Esprit et vie* 86 (1976): 65–71, 97–107, 113–20, at 65 and 120. A portion of this article (pp. 66–68) was translated under the title "The Necessity of Evangelization for the Salvation of the World," *Christ to the World* 21 (1976): 262–66.

15. Robert Rweyemamu, "Il Linguaggio della Chiesa missionaria," *Annuncio*, 195–222, at 222. The author is here alluding to *EN* 2.

16. Salvatore Meo, "Maria Stella dell'Evangelizzazione," *Annuncio*, 763–78. at 763.

17. Jesus Lopez-Gay, "The First Anniversary of Paul VI's…*Evangelization in the Modern World*," *L'Osservatore Romano* (Weekly Edition, 18 December 1976), 7–8, at 8.

18. Dorr, "Reflections on Pope Paul's Document," 538–39.

19. LaVerdiere, "A Scriptural Meditation," 11.

20. Alvin A. Illig, "*Evangelii Nuntiandi*," *National Catholic Reporter*, 1 September 1978, 13.

21. Pedro Arrupe, "Epilogo," in *Evangelii Nuntiandi e la Compagnia di Gesù* (Rome: Centrum Ignatianum Spiritualitatis, 1978), 151–53, at 151. See also Jesus Lopez-Gay, "The First Anniversary," 7; and Pietro Chiocchetta, "Chiesa Evangelizzata Evangelizzatrice," in *Annuncio* 123–68, at 124–25.

22. Delhaye, "Évangélisation chrétienne," 66.

23. José Saraiva Martins, "Nuovo Concetto di Evangelizzazione secondo il Sinodo e la *Evangelii nuntiandi*," *Annuncio*, 59–88, at 61–64, 88.

24. Lopez-Gay, "The First Anniversary," 7.

25. Antonio Furiola, "A Dieci Anni dalla *Evangelii Nuntiandi* Nota Ascetico-Pastorale," *Euntes Docete* 38 (1985): 99–114.

26. E. Testa, "L'Evangelizzazione nelle Sacre Scritture," *Annuncio*, 5–18, at 5. LaVerdiere remarks on the profoundly biblical inspiration of chapters I and VII of *EN* ("Scriptural Meditation," 11). Stefano Virgulin observes that Paul is cited with great frequency, "L'Apostolo Paolo Modello dell'Evangelizzazione," *Annuncio*, 19–33, at 19.

27. Chiocchetta, "Chiesa Evangelizzata," 151.

28. Mario Puccinelli, "Catechesi Via dell'Evangelizzazione," *Annuncio*, 539–54.

29. Robert J. Hater, *The Relationship between Evangelization and Catechesis: A Clarification Paper* (Washington, DC: National Conference of Diocesan Directors of Religious Education, 1981). Twenty-six pages long.

30. Josef Amstutz, "Auftrag der Kirche: Evangelisation und Befreiung," *Neue Zeitschrift für Missionswissenschaft* 32 (1976): 255–79.

31. Delhaye, "Évangélisation chrétinne," 67; English translation in *Christ to the World* 21 (1976): 265.

32. André Seumois, "Communità ecclesiali de base e missioni," *Annuncio*, 343–63, esp. 343.

33. Ermanno Ancilli, "Il Servizio ecclesiale e missionario della vita religiosa," *Annuncio*, 429–62, at 438; compare *EN* 69. See also the fine reflections in Ary-Athanasius Roest Crollius, "Evangelizzazione e Testimonianza di Vita Evangelica," in *EN e la Compagnia di Gesù*, 113–27.

34. Hervé Carrier, *Evangelizing the Culture of Modernity* (Maryknoll, N.Y.: Orbis, 1993), 26. See also Carrier's *Gospel Message and Human Cultures from Leo XIII to John Paul II* (Pittsburgh: Duquesne University Press, 1989), 22.

35. André Joos, "Incontro tra il Messaggio Evangelico e la Cultura alla Luce di Alcuni Orientamenti Teologici del XX Secolo," *Annuncio*, 255–323. On the same theme see also Otto Bischofberger, "Die Evangelisierung der Kulturen," in *Neue Zeitschrift für Missionswissenschaft* 32 (1976): 315–23. This article holds that

EN, without solving the problem of the unity of the gospel and the variety of cultures, takes a positive step forward.

36. Miller, "*EN* and the Parish Priest," 56–57.

37. Fritz Kollbrunner, "Missionstheoretische Überlegungen zu *Evangelii Nuntiandi*," *Neue Zeitschrift für Missionswissenschaft* 32 (1976): 242–54, at 247–48.

38. Domenico Spada, "I Laici e la loro missione nelo sviluppo della moderna teologia," *Annuncio*, 365–415.

39. Editorial signed by Norbert Greinacher and Alois Müller in *Evangelization in the World Today*, Concilium 114 (New York: Seabury/Crossroad, 1979), viii.

40. Michael Singleton and Henri Maurier, "The Establishment's Efforts to Solve the Evangelical Energy Crisis: The Fourth Roman Synod and *Evangelii Nuntiandi*," *Evangelization in the World Today*, 113–19; quotations from 113 and 117.

41. Tihon, "Des missions à la mission," 704.

42. Roger D. Haight, "The 'Established' Church as Mission: The Relation of the Church to the Modern World," *Jurist* 19 (Winter/Spring 1979): 4–39; David Bohr, "Evangelization: The Essential and Primary Mission of the Church," ibid., 40–87. Haight opts for a narrow definition that would treat evangelization as one aspect of mission, pp. 12–13, 21–27. Bohr, following *EN*, argues for a broad concept of evangelization.

43. Berard L. Marthaler, "Evangelization and Catechesis: Word, Memory, Witness," *Living Light* 16 (1979): 33–45, at 34.

44. Snijders, "Movement of Minds," 171. He is referring to *EN* 51.

45. Kohlbrunner, "Missionstheoretische Überlegungen," 243–45.

46. Johannes van der Ven, "The Future of the Church as an Intergenerative Problem," in *The Transmission of the Faith to the Next Generation*, eds. Norbert Greinacher and Virgil Elizondo, Concilium 174 (Edinburgh: T. & T. Clark, 1984), 31–38, at 35. This article, at least in the English version, is very difficult to understand.

47. Jacques Dupuis, SJ, *Jesus Christ and the Encounter of World Religions* (Maryknoll, NY: Orbis, 1991), 218–19.

48. Michael L. Fitzgerald, "La *Evangelii Nuntiandi* e le Religioni del Mondo," in *Annuncio*, 609–67, esp. 614–20 and 626.

49. Kollbrunner, "Missionstheoretische Überlegungen," 250–51.

50. Dorr, "Reflections on Pope Paul's Document," 535.

51. Tihon, "Des missions à la mission," 704.

52. Dorr, "Reflections on Pope Paul's Document," 531.

53. Bischofberger, "Evangelisierung der Kulturen," 323.

54. Fitzgerald, "La *EN* e le Religioni del Mondo," 625; Cf. Snijders, "Movement of Minds," 175.

55. Benno Baumeister and Hans Schmidt, "Basis Gemeinschaft —ein Erfahrungsbericht," written in cooperation with a group of White Fathers, *Neue Zeitschrift für Missionswissenschaft* 32 (1976): 324–41, at 340–41. Dorr, "Reflections on Pope Paul's Document," 538, makes a similar comment.

56. Van der Ven, "Future of the Church," 38.

57. Dorr, "Reflections on Pope Paul's Document," 534, referring to *EN* 37.

58. Francisco Ivern, "Problemi nella Promozione della Giustizia Oggi," in *"Evangelii Nuntiandi" e la Compagnia di Gesù*, 93–111, at 98–99. Ivern's critique at this point resembles that implied in the concluding section of Giuseppe de Rosa's article in *Civiltà cattolica*, mentioned in note 7 above.

59. Ibid., 109.

60. Paul Valladier, "L'Évangélisation dans le monde moderne," 605–10.

61. I borrow the term *crosscurrents* from Louis L. Luzbetak, "The Beneficiaries of Evangelization," in *Catholic Evangelization Today*, 69–83. Luzbetak here uses it to designate theologians who question the necessity of evangelizing adherents of other religions.

62. Robert C. Garafalo, "Evangelization in Crisis," *Communio: International Catholic Review* 16 (1989) 573–93.

63. *Go and Make Disciples: A National Plan and Strategy for Catholic Evangelization* (Washington, DC: Office for Publishing and Promotion Services, 1993); also in *Origins* 22 (December 3, 1992): 423–32. For commentary see Cyprian Davis, "Evangelization in the United States since Vatican Council II," in *Catholic*

Evangelization Today, 22–37; also Kenneth G. Boyack, "Go and Make Disciples: The United States Bishops' National Plan for Catholic Evangelization," in *Pope John Paul II and the New Evangelization*, eds. Ralph Martin and Peter Williamson (San Francisco: Ignatius, 1994), 71–85.

64. Study edition, published 1987 by the Society for the Propagation of the Faith, New York, NY.

65. John Paul II, *Crossing the Threshold of Hope* (New York: Knopf, 1994), 114.

Chapter 3

The Program: Paul VI, John Paul II, and the New Evangelization

Thus far, I have described the reactions to Paul VI's program for evangelization, but I have said little about the contents of this program. It can, I believe, be most opportunely discussed in connection with John Paul II's program for a new evangelization, which follows closely the ideas of his predecessor. Cardinal Wojtyla was an eager participant in the Synod of Bishops of 1974, which prepared materials for Paul VI's apostolic exhortation. As pope, he sought to carry out the programs of Vatican II and Paul VI, the sources from which he draws the principal elements of his program of evangelization. In his many speeches, encyclicals, and other documents, he gave further clarity and precision to what is involved. Evangelization, he asserted, is "the primary service which the Church can render to every individual and to all humanity in the modern world" (*RMis* 2). He, in fact, made himself the principal evangelizer of his day. "The Lord and Master of history," he said in 1990, "has wished my pontificate to be that of a pilgrim pope, walking down the roads of the world, bringing to all peoples the message of salvation."[1]

John Paul II first mentioned the "new evangelization" in a speech at Port-au-Prince, Haiti, on May 9, 1983. The fifth centenary of the first evangelization of the Americas (1492–1992), he declared, should mark the beginning of a new era of evangelization, "new in ardor, methods, and expression." This proposal, often repeated in papal utterances since 1983, gives rise to the questions I shall address in this chapter: What is distinctive to the new evangelization? What did Paul VI and John Paul II respectively contribute toward it? And how was it related to the great jubilee of the year 2000?

In the very first sentence of its *Dogmatic Constitution on the Church*, Vatican II affirmed that Christ had sent the Church to preach the gospel to every creature (*LG* 1; cf. Mark 16:15). Since the Church is missionary by her very nature, said the Council, the task of evangelization is incumbent on every Christian (*LG* 16–17; cf. *AG* 23, 35). The bishops, in union with the pope, are charged with leading the process (*LG* 23; *CD* 6; *AG* 29, 30). Priests are to stir up zeal for evangelization (*PO* 4; *AG* 39), and all the laity are expected to cooperate in this effort, especially in the environments of their work and family life (*LG* 35; *AA* 2, 3, 6; *AG* 41).

With the help of this background, it may be possible to summarize under ten headings some defining traits of the new evangelization. In each case the new trend was introduced by Vatican II and further clarified by Paul VI and John Paul II. The latter did not invent the concept of the "new evangelization," but he promoted it in enormously effective ways.

1. Centrality of Christ. Vatican II, with its program of *ressourcement*, sought to speak in biblical language and to focus on Christ, the light of the world, whose radiance sustains the Church. It recognized a "hierarchy of truths," in which the Lordship of Christ the Son of God stands at the highest level (*UR* 11).

Paul VI spoke often of the centrality of Jesus Christ. "There can be no true evangelization," he wrote, "if the name, the teaching, the life, the promises, the kingdom and the mystery of Jesus of Nazareth the Son of God, are not proclaimed" (*EN* 22; cf. 27). After quoting Paul VI to this effect, John Paul II states that all missionary proclamation must have its center in Christ (*RMis* 44). On another occasion he declares: "The new evangelization begins with the clear and emphatic proclamation of the gospel, which is directed to each and every person. Therefore it is necessary to awaken again in believers a full relationship with Christ, mankind's only Savior. Only from a personal relationship with Jesus can an effective evangelization develop."[2]

If this aspect of evangelization was put into practice, the Catholic Church might keep pace with Protestant Evangelicals in her missionary expansion. There would be no occasion for Catholics to leave their Church and join fundamentalist or Pentecostal communities on the ground that Catholicism gave them no sense of being personally related to the Lord.

2. **Ecumenism**. The new evangelization, unlike most of the Catholic preaching since the Reformation, is ecumenical. In line with Vatican II, the recent popes have called attention to the authentic elements of faith in other Christian communities. They are seriously committed to promoting the unity of all Christians in accordance with the high-priestly prayer of Jesus (John 17:20–25).

Vatican II in its *Decree on Ecumenism* called upon all Christians to bear witness to their common hope (*UR* 12) without falling into false conciliatory approaches (*UR* 11). It noted that the lack of unity among Christians seriously damages the witness of the Church (*UR* 1). Paul VI and John Paul II frequently repeated this important observation. Paul VI called upon all Christians to give greater common witness to Christ before the world when they engage in missionary proclamation (*EN* 77).

John Paul II asked how it is possible to proclaim the gospel of reconciliation without at the same time being concerned for reconciliation among Christians (*UUS* 98). The very name of Christ, which is the focus of evangelization, should draw Christians together. The spread of what John Paul calls "para-Christian sects" makes it more urgent than ever, in his estimation, for different churches and ecclesial communities to bear harmonious witness to Christ (*RMis* 50). But he insisted that the existing differences must be honestly faced. "The obligation to respect the truth is absolute" (*UUS* 79).

3. **Interreligious Dialogue**. The necessary relationship of evangelization to interreligious dialogue has been strongly emphasized in the past two generations. Some missionaries are suspicious of dialogue because it seems to undermine evangelization, and conversely, some proponents of dialogue feel that their efforts are impeded by any intent to evangelize. Yet Vatican II, while strongly urging the missionary imperative, encouraged dialogue and collaboration with followers of other religions (*AG* 41; *NA* 2).

Paul VI and John Paul II found no conflict between authentic dialogue and proclamation. Having emphasized the need for mutual respect and dialogue in his encyclical *Ecclesiam suam* (*ES* 81, 112), Paul VI in *Evangelii nuntiandi* warned that esteem for other religions should not lead us to refrain from proclaiming Jesus Christ (*EN* 53; cf. *ES* 82).

John Paul II made similar points. The assurance of possessing universally valid truths is not an obstacle but a help to sincere and authentic dialogue (*FR* 92). An honest dialogue requires the parties to trust one another and to speak frankly about their differences. Because Christians who engage in dialogue must declare their own faith, dialogue includes proclamation as an integral part. Proclamation itself must be carried on in a spirit of dialogue, with respect for the conscience of the other party and a ready willingness to learn (*RMis* 55–57).

4. Religious Freedom. In centuries past, moral and physical force were sometimes used to induce people to accept the true faith. The new evangelization, by contrast, presupposes full acceptance of Vatican II's *Declaration on Religious Freedom*, which taught that people should be encouraged to follow their free and responsible judgment, without external pressure (*DH* 1). Paul VI in *Evangelii nuntiandi* taught that the Church should propose the truth of the gospel without seeking to impose anything on the consciences of the hearers (*EN* 80). Echoing this thought, John Paul II declared: "The Church proposes; she imposes nothing" (*RMis* 39). Recognizing that the assent of faith must by its very nature be free, the Church avoids offensive proselytization. She proclaims the gospel in a way that honors the sanctuary of every human conscience (*RMis* 8, 39). The acceptance of Christ, far from diminishing freedom, fulfills it, according to the saying of Jesus, "The truth shall make you free" (John 8:32).

5. Continuing Process. Evangelization has often been restrictively understood as though it meant only the first proposal of the gospel to people who had not as yet heard it. Vatican II used the noun *evangelizatio* only rarely (e.g., *CD* 6; *AA* 6; *AG* 38) and then chiefly as a synonym for the initial "proclamation of the gospel" ("*nuntium evangelicum*," *AG* 10). But it sometimes used the term in a broader sense that would seem to include interaction between the gospel and the local culture (*GS* 44).

[margin handwritten note: coerced / imposed; faith is never imposed, it is proposed]

[handwritten note: evangelization of cultures]

Paul VI in *Evangelii nuntiandi* spelled out a very comprehensive conception of evangelization, including the ministry of preaching and sacraments and indeed the whole process by which human life is penetrated and transformed by the gospel (*EN* 14; 17–18). Pastoral care of the faithful, therefore, is a matter of continuing evangelization. The Church herself, he explained, is in constant need of being evangelized (*EN* 15).

John Paul II, building on these insights, distinguished three phases of evangelization. "First evangelization," in his terminology, is missionary proclamation in regions where Christ is still unknown or where the Church has not yet taken root. The second phase, continuing evangelization, consists in the pastoral care of Christians who are seeking to put their lives more fully under the influence of the gospel. Finally, the process includes the reevangelization of those who have fallen away or allowed their faith to grow cold (*RMis* 33). The viability of communities of faith is put to the test in situations of hedonistic consumerism or grinding poverty. In these situations, reevangelization will involve an overcoming of the separation between the gospel and daily life in family, work, and society (*CL* 34).

6. Social Teaching. In past centuries, it became customary to draw a sharp line of demarcation between the spiritual realm, which was that of the Church and eternal life, and the temporal realm, which belonged to the state and worldly institutions. In this framework, evangelization was seen as speaking to people's inner life with a view to their eternal salvation. The Church, to be sure, was deeply engaged in corporal works of mercy, including charity toward the sick and the poor, but these charitable activities were distinguished from evangelization.

In the twentieth century, it became increasingly clear that authentic conversion includes a commitment to the common good. The 1971 Synod of Bishops made the famous statement: "Action on behalf of justice and participation in the transformation of the world fully appear to us as a constitutive dimension of the preaching of the gospel or, in other words, of the Church's mission for the redemption of the human race and its liberation from every oppressive situation" (*JW* 6). The Church has a responsibility, said the Synod, to witness before the world that the gospel message contains clear imperatives to work for peace and justice in society (*JW* 36).

Paul VI took up the socioeconomic aspects of evangelization in an important section of *Evangelii nuntiandi*. He affirmed the importance of denouncing oppressive and dehumanizing structures as antithetical to the gospel itself. But he also warned against the temptation to reduce the Church's mission to that of a purely temporal project. Priority, he said, must always be given to the religious finality of evangelization and to the interior conversion that is required for salvation (*EN* 32–35). No social structures can assure a truly human culture, he said, unless the rulers and the people have undergone a conversion of mind and heart (*EN* 36).

John Paul II frequently returned to the same theme. His position was substantially that of Paul VI. "Authentic human development," he wrote, "must be rooted in an ever deeper evangelization" (*RMis* 58). At the Puebla Conference of the Latin American bishops in 1979, he said: "If the Church makes herself present in the defense of or in the advancement of man, she does so in line with her mission, which although it is religious and not social or political, cannot fail to consider man in the entirety of his being."[3]

A social system in which some are lured into ruthless competition for wealth and luxury, while others are driven into abject poverty, is contrary to the vision of society held forth by the gospel. Evangelization must therefore include determined efforts to build a civilization of peace, solidarity, and love. Total or integral evangelization will inevitably "penetrate deeply into social and cultural reality, including the economic and political order."[4] Pope John Paul saw his program of human rights as a vital component of the new evangelization.

7. **Evangelization of Cultures**. In the past, evangelization has generally been understood rather narrowly as consisting in the direct proclamation of the gospel. Without neglecting the importance of personal conversion, the new evangelization takes cognizance of the general cultural setting. As Paul VI explained in an important section of *Evangelii nuntiandi*, evangelization is often impeded by an unwholesome split between faith and culture. Cultures themselves need to be "regenerated by an encounter with the gospel" (*EN* 20).

John Paul II spoke frequently of the evangelization of cultures and of the necessary dialogue between faith and cultures. While cultures serve the gospel by supplying the necessary means of expression and communication, cultures themselves can be interiorly purified, elevated, and transformed by openness to Christian faith and values. As explained in *Centesimus annus*, evangelization "plays a role in the culture of various nations, sustaining culture in its progress toward truth and assisting in the work of its purification and enrichment" (*CA* 50). Where the prevailing culture remains closed and hostile, faith cannot fully express itself, nor can the culture achieve its full potential. To overcome these difficulties the Church must seek methods of proposing the gospel that are effective in the existing culture. Without dilution or distortion, the Christian message has to be integrated as far as possible into the "new culture" created by modern technology (*RMis* 37c). In his later encyclical on faith and reason, the pope calls for greater attention to philosophy as a service to the new evangelization. The word of God, he asserts, gives access to new dimensions of the true, the good, and the beautiful (*FR* 103).

8. New Media. Still another characteristic of the new evangelization, mentioned by John Paul II in his Port-au-Prince speech, is its employment of new methods and expressions. Vatican II had already spoken of the need to use the new instruments of social communication in preaching the good news of redemption (*IM* 3). Paul VI in his apostolic exhortation noted that since our age is deeply influenced by the mass media, evangelization must make use of these channels. "The Church would feel guilty before the Lord if she did not utilize these powerful means that human skill is daily rendering more perfect" (*EN* 45). But he added that public proclamation cannot take the place of person-to-person contact, which remains indispensable for touching and transforming consciences (*EN* 46).

Here again, John Paul II followed in the footsteps of his predecessor. "The evangelization of modern culture," he declared, "depends to a great extent on the influence of the media" (*RMis* 37c). Elsewhere he wrote: "The world of mass communications represents a new frontier for the mission of the Church because it is undergoing a rapid and innovative development and has an extensive worldwide influence on the formation of mentality and customs" (*CL* 44).

St. Paul saw the necessity of proclaiming the gospel at the cultural center of the ancient world—the Areopagus of Athens. In a similar way, John Paul II contends, the world of the mass media constitutes a new Areopagus, which the Church must not neglect. It is insufficient, he said, simply to use new techniques of dissemination; the message itself must be integrated into the new styles of thought and expression, the "psychology" of the new cultural sectors (*RMis* 37c). Radio, television, and computer technology must not be allowed to dictate the message but must be prudently employed to open new avenues of access to the gospel. The Catholic Church, with its rich patrimony of art, architecture, music, and ritual is in some ways extraordinarily well suited to the electronic media. John Paul II used these media effectively in televised liturgies, but he recognized that esthetic delight does not amount to personal conversion. Because faith and holiness are always essential, he wrote, the true missionary is the saint (*RMis* 90).

9. <u>Involvement of All Christians</u>. As noted earlier in this chapter, evangelization has often been seen in the past as the special concern of apostolic associations of priests and members of missionary orders. While recognizing the unique role played by religious communities, the Second Vatican Council insisted that the whole Church is missionary, and that "the work of evangelization is a basic duty of the People of God" (*AG* 35). The laity, incorporated in Christ by baptism, confirmation, and the Eucharist, are in duty bound to cooperate in the expansion and growth of Christ's Body (*AG* 36; cf. *LG* 16–17).

Ten years after the Council, Paul VI pointed out that "it is the whole Church that receives the mission to evangelize" (*EN* 15). Toward the end of *Evangelii nuntiandi*, he distinguished among the respective responsibilities of the pope, the bishops, priests, religious, and laity (*EN* 66–73).

John Paul II made similar distinctions. Bishops, he says, "are the pillars on which rest the work and the responsibility of evangelization, which has as its purpose the building up of the Body of Christ."[5] Priests, he held, are by vocation "responsible for awakening the missionary consciousness of the faithful."[6] Members of religious orders and congregations can play a special role because of their total gift of self through the vows of chastity, poverty, and obedience, which dramatically attest to the values of the kingdom of God (*RMis* 69; cf. *VC* 87–92).

In his apostolic exhortation on the laity, the late pope called attention to the duty of lay Christians to make their daily conduct a shining and convincing testimony to the gospel (*CL* 34, 51). It is their special responsibility, he said, to demonstrate how Christian faith constitutes the only fully valid response to the problems and hopes that life presents to every person and society (*CL* 34).

In his apostolic exhortation on the family, John Paul II included a section on the family as an evangelizing community in which the members evangelize one another as well as other families. Parents, he taught, are the first evangelizers of their children (*FC* 51–54).

10. Primacy of the Holy Spirit. From some earlier presentations of evangelization and missionary activity, one might get the impression that, while the Holy Spirit inspired the apostles, apostolic activity in subsequent generations depends on merely human initiative. The new evangelization, avoiding any such crypto-Pelagianism, explicitly calls attention to the continuing role of the Spirit.

Vatican II, in its *Decree on the Church's Missionary Activity*, pointed out that the Holy Spirit unceasingly accompanies and directs the Church in its salvific labors (*AG* 4). Paul VI carried this theme forward in *Evangelii nuntiandi*. "The Holy Spirit," he wrote, "is the principal agent of evangelization: it is he who impels each individual to proclaim the gospel, and it is he who in the depths of consciences causes the word of salvation to be accepted and understood" (*EN* 75).

John Paul II in *Redemptoris missio* has an entire chapter bearing the title "The Holy Spirit: The Principal Agent of Mission." Without recourse to the Spirit, he writes, we cannot have the wisdom, enthusiasm, courage, and convincing power that enables us to pass on our experience of Jesus and the hope that motivates us (*RMis* 24). And in another context he writes: "Missionary dynamism is not born of the will of those who decide to become propagators of their faith. It is born of the Spirit, who moves the

principle agent
of the NE =
The HS

38

Church to expand, and it progresses through faith in God's love."[7] The new evangelization, as both these popes understand it, relies less on human plans and projections than on the unforeseeable initiatives of the Holy Spirit.

John Paul II, at the beginning of his pontificate, pointed out that with the approach of the year 2000 the Church was already in the season of a new Advent, a time to render thanks for past favors and to ask God's blessing on the years to come. Since the Marian Year of 1987, and especially since 1990, he linked the great Jubilee with the new evangelization. These Advent years, he declared, should be the occasion of an examination of conscience regarding the extent to which the Church of the past millennium has been faithful to her mission. As the Church enters the third millennium of her existence, he asked, can she give a good account of her fidelity to her mandate?

In discerning the signs of the present time, John Paul expressed his conviction that evangelization is more urgent than ever, for the number of people who do not know Christ has practically doubled since the close of Vatican II (*RMis* 3). Seeking to escape from the dehumanizing pressures of technology and consumerism and from the barren agnosticism of the prevalent philosophies, many are hungering for richer spiritual nourishment. New opportunities for evangelization are offered by the rapidity of travel and by instant communications. Certain gospel values, such as those of human dignity and freedom, have become part of the universal patrimony of all peoples. The year 1989 witnessed the collapse of some oppressive regimes that were blocking the spread of the gospel. As the millennium drew to a close, the pope felt authorized to declare: "God is opening before the Church the horizons of a new humanity more fully prepared for the sowing of the gospel. I sense that the moment has come to commit all the Church's energies to a new evangelization and to the mission *ad gentes*. No believer in Christ, no institution of the Church can avoid this supreme duty: to proclaim Christ to all peoples" (*RMis* 3).

Pope John Paul II frequently linked the program of the new evangelization to the advent of the new millennium. "As the third millennium of the redemption draws near, God is preparing a great springtime for Christianity, and we can already see its first signs"

(*RMis* 86). But after the turn of the millennium Pope John Paul continued to speak of the new evangelization, as may be seen from the apostolic letter *Novo millennio ineunte*. In that letter he declares: "A new millennium is opening before the Church like a vast ocean upon which we shall venture, relying on the help of Christ....The missionary mandate accompanies us into the Third Millennium...." (*NMI* 58). The program, therefore, was by no means limited to the closing years of the twentieth century.

At this point, it might seem logical to add a chapter on Benedict XVI and the new evangelization, but at the present stage of the new pontificate such a chapter would be at least premature. Pope Benedict does, to be sure, speak of evangelization as the first and foremost task of the Church. In his trip to the United States in April 2008, several times he mentioned the new evangelization. In his homily at St. Patrick's Cathedral in New York, he implored from God the grace of a new Pentecost and spoke of a new springtime in the Spirit for the Church in America. In countless books, articles, speeches, and homilies he performs the work of evangelization. But he has not made the new evangelization a major theme of his pontificate, as his predecessor did. He is on guard against raising false hopes of mass conversions to the faith. Temperamentally he is more reserved than John Paul II, but he shares similar hopes and objectives regarding the new evangelization.

Notes

1. John Paul II, Arrival Speech in Mexico City, May 6, 1990; *ORE*, May 7, 1990, pp. 1 and 12.

2. Ad Limina visit of Bishops of Southern Germany, December 4, 1992; *ORE*, December 23–30, 1992, pp. 5–6, at 5.

3. John Paul II, Address to General Assembly of Latin American Bishops at Puebla, III, 2; *Origins* 8 (February 8, 1979): 529–38, at 536.

4. Ad Limina visit of Puerto Rico bishops, October 27, 1988; *ORE* December 5, 1988, pp. 7 and 14, at 14.

5. John Paul II, "Address to Italian Bishops' Conference," May 18, 1989; *ORE* June 5, 1989, pp. 7 and 16, at 16.

6. John Paul II, "Message for World Mission Day," October 21, 1990; *ORE* June 11, 1990, p. 9.

7. John Paul II, Address of February 12, 1988 to Italian Bishops on Liturgical Course, *ORE* March 14, 1988, p. 5.

Chapter 4

The Gospel: Point of Contention and Convergence

The term *evangelization* means "the dissemination of the gospel." It is therefore important for our purposes to know what is meant by the gospel. Different conceptions of its meaning have been operative since the debate between Lutherans and Catholics in the sixteenth century.

Erasmus, who seems to have coined the term *evangelical*, used it to disparage what he regarded as the narrowness and fanaticism of the Lutherans. Luther did not call himself an evangelical, but he did regard the gospel (*evangelium*) as the heart of the Christian reality. He developed a highly personal conception of the gospel based on his own religious pilgrimage.

Convinced that he could not be anything else but a sinner, Luther despaired of being made righteous through observance of the commandments. Even his good works, he felt, were contaminated by his sinful motives and dispositions and thus fell short of the purity that God required. Through meditation on the New Testament, however, he discovered to his relief that even sinners could be saved. Paul, he believed, taught that the true path to salvation was through faith in Christ, whose merits would be imputed to all who put their trust in him. If we would only cling to Christ in faith, God would declare us righteous in spite of our faults.

The gospel, for Luther, was not a book. The four books called Gospels, he pointed out, are four versions of the one gospel. That gospel is a message to be proclaimed—primarily by word of mouth and secondarily through the sacraments. Christian proclamation includes two basic elements, law and gospel. The law, which tells us what we ought to do, burdens us with a sense of obligation and of guilt for our failure to observe it. It thus prepares us to receive with joy the good news that God forgives us, in spite of our sins, provided that we put our faith in Christ. Evangelization, therefore, means for Lutherans the dissemination of the gospel as the good news of forgiveness and salvation through faith in Christ.

The Catholic understanding of the gospel, and consequently of evangelization, differs in some respects from Luther's. It was formally articulated by the Council of Trent, which met shortly after Luther's death. That Council, like Luther, used the term "gospel" in the singular to mean the message to be proclaimed. Like Luther, again, Trent held that the gospel, foretold by the prophets of ancient Israel, was promulgated by Christ himself, who commanded the apostles to preach the gospel they had learned from him and from the Holy Spirit. This gospel, moreover, was "the source of all saving truth and moral instruction" (*DS* 1501).

A major difference from Luther appears at this point. For Trent, the gospel is not only the promise of forgiveness but also the source of doctrinal truth and moral instruction. It tells us what we are to believe on God's word and what we are to do. In laying down the rules whereby Christians are to regulate their lives, the gospel functions, to some extent, as law. In its *Decree on Justification*, the council rejected what it understood as the Lutheran view. Let me quote two of the condemned propositions:

"Canon 19. If anyone says that in the gospel nothing but faith is prescribed, while other matters are indifferent, neither prescribed nor forbidden, but free; or that the Ten Commandments in no way apply to Christians; let him be anathema" (*DS* 1569).

"Canon 20. If anyone says that a justified person, of whatever degree of perfection, is not bound to keep the commandments of God and of the Church but only to believe, as if the gospel were simply a bare and unqualified promise of eternal life without the condition of observing the commandments; let him be anathema" (*DS* 1570).

We need not decide here whether these canons reflect the real teaching of Luther, the mistaken views of some of Luther's followers, or Catholic misrepresentations of the Lutheran position. In any case, they help us to understand the Catholic point of view. For

Catholics the gospel does not unconditionally promise eternal life to all who believe. Rather, it offers a firm hope of salvation to believers who, relying on the help of grace, strive to observe God's law, including the Ten Commandments. This requirement, of course, does not cancel out God's promise of mercy toward sinners and God's readiness to forgive those who sincerely repent of their failures and resolve to amend their ways. The doctrine of forgiveness, a central feature of the gospel, is amply set forth at various points in Trent's *Decree on Justification*.

During the two centuries following the Council of Trent, Catholics reacting against what they understood as Protestant errors, showed a marked tendency to emphasize the element of obligation. They rarely used the terms *gospel* and *evangelization*, which sounded too Protestant to their ears. Falling into a kind of legalism, some Catholics depicted the Church more as a divine law-enforcement agency than as a refuge for repentant sinners and a herald of good tidings. Revelation and Church doctrine were frequently portrayed as a set of obligatory rules and tenets over and above the deliverances of unaided reason.

From the sixteenth century to the middle of the twentieth, it was widely supposed that a choice had to be made between two mutually antithetical forms of Christianity: the evangelical and the catholic. The evangelical model emphasized the primacy of the Bible as the word of God, the urgency of proclamation, and justification by faith alone. The catholic model focused on Church tradition, sacramental mediation, and good works. This contrast was not without a basis in fact. The Protestant Reformation had been a reaction against the exorbitant sacramentalism and legalism of the late Middle Ages. The Catholic Reformation (or Counter-Reformation, as some call it) reacted in turn against the narrow biblicism and fideism that it discerned in Protestantism. Reacting against each other, the two forms of Western Christianity progressively diverged in the next few centuries.

Although the differences were real and serious, the resulting antithesis was too simplistic to endure. From the Protestant side, reflective believers found that Scripture could not stand alone. The Bible itself was a crystallization of pre-Christian and apostolic tradition under the aegis of the Holy Spirit. The New Testament itself called for authoritative transmission of pure doctrine under the leadership of duly appointed leaders. It attached great importance to ritual actions such as baptism, the Lord's Supper, the anointing of the sick, and the laying on of hands for ministry. Not content with faith alone, Christ and the apostles taught the necessity of obedience to the moral law, reaffirming and radicalizing the Ten Commandments.

Protestants increasingly recognized that it was no longer possible to go back to the Bible alone. Every Christian community inevitably read the Bible through the lens of some tradition. The slogan "Scripture alone" was itself a tradition rather than a biblical doctrine. The Bible was an excellent and irreplaceable instrument for communicating the faith, but it was never intended to support the full weight of being the source and norm of all that claimed to be Christian. Transmitted within the tradition of the Church, the Bible needed to be clarified by creedal and dogmatic assertions in order to be protected against abuse.

Protestants who were sensitive to these inescapable facts felt a keen desire to recover the heritage that their churches had partly lost. Especially when they began to read the giants of the patristic age—such as Ignatius, Irenaeus, Clement of Alexandria, Athanasius, the Cappadocian Fathers, the two Cyrils, Hilary, Ambrose, Augustine, and Leo—they found their faith strengthened and enriched. They experienced deeper communion with fellow Christians and found a spiritual home much warmer and more inviting than the bare text that the Bible supplied. A number of Protestant churches began to describe themselves not simply as evangelical or reformed but as "evangelical and catholic" or in some cases as "evangelical, catholic, and reformed."

On the Catholic side, a corresponding movement in the opposite direction was occurring. Many of the faithful began to grow restive under the weight of ecclesiastical dogmas, laws, and traditions that had become rigid and opaque with the passage of time. Obedience to Church authority, they found, could easily become too passive and mechanical, as though it could relieve individuals of personal responsibility. They felt the hunger for a simpler and more focused faith and for more spontaneous styles of community life. Theologians began to call for *ressourcement*, a conscious effort to renew the Church by reappropriating the freshness and enthusiasm of apostolic and patristic Christianity. In so doing they gained a more positive appreciation for what Luther and the early Protestant Reformers had in mind.

As a result of the tendencies I have described, a number of new movements arose in the churches, both Protestant and Catholic. Biblical movements, kerygmatic movements, and liturgical movements bridged over the denominational chasms and fed into the ecumenical movement of the twentieth century.

The future Pope John XXIII encountered these movements of renewal at first hand during his years as apostolic nuncio in France. In convoking the Second Vatican Council, he gave them a great opportunity to revitalize the whole Church. The Council, as we know, presented Catholic doctrine in a style that was biblical and ecumenical, seeking to foster solidarity with Protestants and other persons of good will.

In a sentence that the Protestant theologian Oscar Cullmann singled out as supremely important in the Council's documentation, the *Decree on Ecumenism* declared that revealed truths differed from one another in importance: "When comparing doctrines they [theologians] should remember that in Catholic teaching there exists an order or 'hierarchy' of truths, since they vary in their relationship to the foundation of the Christian faith" (*UR* 11).

Early in the next paragraph the decree invited all Christians to profess together "their faith in God, one and three, and in the incarnate Son of God, our Redeemer and Lord. United in their efforts, and with mutual respect, let them bear witness to our common hope, which does not play us false" (*UR* 12). In these crucial sentences, the Second Vatican Council lent its support to an ecumenical program of evangelization that would be centered on the heart of the gospel message.

The recent popes have shown how this new style of gospel-centered evangelization can be authentically Catholic. Paul VI did so in his apostolic exhortation of 1975, *Evangelii nuntiandi*. John Paul II did the same in many documents, but perhaps especially in his apostolic exhortation for the Americas, *Ecclesia in America* (1999). "The vital core of the new evangelization," he wrote, "must be a clear and unequivocal proclamation of the person of

Jesus Christ, that is, the preaching of his name, his teaching, his life, his promise of the Kingdom which he has gained for us by his Paschal Mystery" (*Ecclesia in America*, 66). He exhorted Catholics to seek living encounters with the Lord in prayer. "To follow Jesus," he declared, "involves living as he lived, accepting his message, adopting his way of thinking, embracing his destiny and sharing his project, which is the plan of the Father....The burning desire to invite others to encounter the One whom we have encountered is the start of the evangelizing mission to which the whole Church is called" (ibid., 68).

In the years following Vatican II, Catholics and Lutherans have gone a long way in resolving their differences about the nature of the gospel. The Joint Lutheran-Catholic Commission, in its Malta Report of 1972, without resolving all differences, described the gospel as "the proclamation of what God has done for the salvation of the world in Jesus Christ" (16). Later Lutheran-Catholic dialogues amplified on the work of Malta.

During the past two decades, significant conversations have taken place between Catholics and Evangelicals. The Evangelical World Fellowship (now known as the World Evangelical Alliance) and the Pontifical Council for Promoting Christian Unity have held a series of consultations since 1993, one result of which is the report "Church, Evangelization, and the Bonds of *Koinonia*," completed in 2002.

In the United States an unofficial group known as Evangelicals and Catholics Together (ECT) has been meeting since 1992 under the joint chairmanship of Charles Colson and Richard John Neuhaus. Its first statement, in 1994, took up the topic of Christian mission with the objective of reducing the tensions that have arisen in Latin America and elsewhere. The participants were able to register their ability to recognize each other as brothers in Christ. In 1997, ECT published under the title "The Gift of Salvation" a declaration that in some ways paralleled the Lutheran-Catholic Joint Declaration on Justification of 1999. In 2002, the same group issued a statement on Scripture and tradition, entitled "Your Word Is Truth." Subsequent statements from ECT have dealt with Christian holiness and with the culture of life, important themes that bond the two groups together.

How far can the holy exchange of gifts go? Can Catholics be fully evangelical and evangelicals be fully catholic? A negative answer would follow if evangelicals are defined as Protestants, since it is impossible to be both Protestant and Catholic at once. But this definition is questionable if not false. Evangelicalism may have originated as a style of Protestantism, but it is no longer a church or a party within a church. It has developed into a movement that is visibly at work in many churches and communions, notably in Anglicanism, Methodism, Reformed churches, Baptists, and Pentecostals.

In the year 2000, the Evangelical cochairman of the International Catholic-Pentecostal Dialogue, Cecil M. Robeck, Jr., proposed to define evangelicalism in terms of three characteristics: acceptance of the gospel as authoritatively defined by Scripture; personal faith in Christ as Lord, and an impulse to communicate the gospel both in evangelism and in social reform.[1] It seems to me that all three of these features can be accepted by Catholics, though not necessarily in the same ways as found in Protestant evangelicalism.

As I have mentioned in my earlier discussion of the Council of Trent, the Catholic Church is committed to the gospel of Christ as the source of all saving truth, though it has not embraced Luther's sharp distinction between law and gospel. Acceptance of the gospel for Catholics involves both trust in Christ's promise of forgiveness and a commitment to embrace the doctrine he taught and the way of life he enjoined on his disciples. Paul himself transcends the opposition between law and gospel when he speaks of being subject to the law of Christ (1 Cor 9:21) and fulfilling the law of Christ (Gal 6:2). The law, therefore, is not simply a threatening demand that convicts us of sin but also a norm by which we may freely model our lives.

Robeck's requirement that evangelicals accept Scripture as authoritatively defining the gospel poses no difficulty for Catholics, who regard the Bible as the inspired word of God. With a few minor exceptions, Protestants and Catholics accept the same Scriptures, but they tend to interpret them somewhat differently. As noted in an earlier section of this chapter, Catholics read Scripture deliberately in the light of Catholic tradition. But this fact cannot preclude them from being evangelicals, because many

Protestant evangelicals agree that Holy Scripture is properly read within the tradition of the Fathers and early councils. Protestants and Catholics are cooperating fruitfully in editing new patristic commentaries on Scripture and writing new studies of the Fathers. Evangelical Christians are in no way bound to play off Scripture against tradition, as was done in some of the polemics of the past.

As the second characteristic of evangelical Christianity, Robeck mentions personal faith in Christ the Lord. Protestant evangelicals are outstanding for their personal commitment to Christ as Lord. But Catholic spiritual leaders agree that such faith is to be assiduously cultivated, even though in many cases it may be lacking. To illustrate how the evangelical leaven is at work in contemporary Catholicism I have already quoted some passages from the apostolic exhortation of John Paul II to the Church in America.

Robeck points out that many Protestant evangelicals interpret the word "personal" individualistically, whereas Catholics are more likely to understand "personal" as implying solidarity with the whole community of believers. The weakness of the Protestant view, he explains, is that it involves "a real concern for 'me and my relationship with Jesus' without an equally strong relationship to my solidarity with my brothers and sisters in Christ." The weakness of the Catholic position, correspondingly, is its tendency "to produce Christians who are willing to rely upon membership in the Church as the means of salvation while taking upon themselves little or no personal responsibility."[2]

Although many exceptions can be found, Robeck's evaluations are probably sound and can for that reason be helpful to Protestants and Catholics alike. Protestants can profitably grow in their appreciation of the communion of the saints, which they confess in the creed. The Catholic Church, for its part, has exceptional resources for cultivating a deeply personal relationship with Christ in personal prayer and in the sacraments. The sacrament of penance requires the penitent to examine his or her personal sins and submit them to the power of the keys. In Holy Communion, Christ gives himself intimately to each individual recipient.

The third point in Robeck's characterization of evangelicalism is "a desire to communicate the gospel truth both in evangelism and social reform."[3] Here, I think, he identifies an area in which notable convergence has already occurred and in which further progress may be expected. Protestant evangelicals of the twentieth century tended to put the accent on evangelism rather than social action, whereas Catholics since Vatican II have given more attention to social justice and liberation than to proclamation.

Protestants can perhaps learn something from the Catholic tradition of social teaching, expressed, for example, in the great social encyclicals. They may consider whether they can find merit in the doctrine of natural law that lies at the basis of much Catholic social teaching. As for Catholics, they would do well to emulate the bold proclamation of Jesus as Lord and Savior that is so prominent in Protestant evangelicalism. Paul VI in *Evangelii nuntiandi* warned against the error of reducing the Church's mission to the dimensions of a simply temporal project (*EN* 32). He called for "a clear and unequivocal proclamation of the Lord Jesus" and stated that there can be no true evangelization if the name of Jesus is not proclaimed (*EN* 22). John Paul II throughout his long pontificate spoke in much the same terms.

Protestant Evangelical and Pentecostal churches are today the fastest growing segments of Christianity. Because of their emphasis on personal faith, they are able to bring a sense of urgency and fervor to contemporary evangelization. Roused by the example of their Protestant counterparts, Catholics may awaken from their evangelical lethargy and proclaim Jesus once again with energy and power. In an article entitled "Why Catholics Should Witness Verbally to the Gospel," Thomas Weinandy, OFM Cap., writes:

> Many contemporary Catholics possess no evangelistic fervor. One reason could be that they have little or no experiential knowledge of Jesus, and may even be ignorant of the basic Gospel message: that Jesus himself is the Good News. Perhaps they simply have not been fully transformed by the power and life of the Holy Spirit that comes through faith in Jesus and thus are incapable of offering this new life to others.[4]

Robeck, after quoting this passage, remarks that Weinandy "sounds very much like an Evangelical." My own thought would be that Catholics can not only speak very like evangelicals but can be evangelical in the full sense of the term. Evangelicalism is not a denomination or a party but a dimension of authentic Christianity insofar as the gospel is the heart of Christian faith.

Let us return to the twofold question whether Catholics can be evangelical and whether evangelicals can be Catholic. In answering the first question, I have to some extent answered the second. The same person can be both catholic and evangelical. To reach that answer I have had to modify the conventional understanding of the term *evangelical* to strip it of its denominational implications and treat it as a generic quality that can and should be present in any body that claims to be Christian.

Can the same be done with the word *catholic?* A difficulty arises from the fact that a particular Christian Church understands itself as the Catholic Church. When I call myself a Catholic, I identify myself as a member of that one church. It would be misleading to call a Protestant a Catholic, since Protestant and Catholic as denominational affiliations are mutually exclusive. In that sense, evangelicals who do not belong to the Catholic Church cannot be Catholic.

For many centuries, however, it has been customary to distinguish two senses of the term *catholic.* Spelled with an uppercase C, it refers to the Catholic Church as a socially organized body. With a lowercase c, however, it designates certain characteristics that can be present in greater or lesser measure in many different churches. In this second sense, churches are catholic to the extent that they are marked by sacred tradition, by sacramental worship, and by ecclesiastical authority. Elements such as these need not be seen as alien to the gospel, as they were by nineteenth-century liberal Protestants. Depending on how the gospel is interpreted, a church may be intensely catholic and at the same time thoroughly evangelical. It will be evangelical because it recognizes the primacy and centrality of Jesus Christ and his redemptive action, while its catholicity will give it plenitude and allow it to transform human lives and cultures. Far from impeding evangelization, the catholic elements may serve to arouse and fortify the evangelical spirit by bringing the faithful into closer union with Jesus Christ, who makes himself present and active through the ministry and sacraments of his Church. The Catholic Church, therefore, need not be any less evangelical than, say, the Assemblies of God, but its evangelicalism will have a different style.

Because evangelicalism and catholicity can reinforce each other, we can without paradox speak of catholic evangelization. Many years before he became a cardinal, Walter Kasper declared that the gospel, according to Holy Scripture, is "the power of the risen Lord in and over the Church through his saving word. The gospel, then, is not a merely historical quantity but a present power, which continually shapes new expression for itself in the confession and witness of the Church without ever exhausting itself in this confession."[5] Imbued with a divine dynamism, the gospel turns individual believers and the Church herself into active carriers of the message. The gospel speaks in and through them. They cannot keep to themselves the faith by which they have been joined to Christ.

Notes

1. Cecil M. Robeck, Jr., "Evangelicals and Catholics Together," in Thomas P. Rausch, ed., *Catholics and Evangelicals: Do They Share a Common Future?* (New York: Paulist, 2000), 13–36, at 18.

2. Ibid., 20.

3. Ibid., 18.

4. Thomas Weinandy in *New Oxford Review* 60 (July/ August 1993): 16, quoted by Robeck, "Evangelicals and Catholics Together," 21.

5. Walter Kasper, *Glaube und Geschichte* (Mainz: Matthias Grünewald, 1970), 199.

Chapter 5

Evangelization and Ecumenism

One might think of ecumenism and evangelization as unrelated, or even as contraries. Ecumenism has to do with relations among Christians, whereas evangelization is thought to be directed toward non-Christians. Ecumenism aims to achieve mutual understanding and agreement, whereas evangelization seeks conversion. For these reasons people frequently suppose that neither ecumenism nor evangelization helps the other.

Historic Links

The opposite, however, is true. The ecumenical movement had its origins in the World Missionary Conference held at Edinburgh in 1910. The two most influential figures at that Conference were probably the American Methodist layman, John R. Mott, and the Canadian-born Anglican bishop, Charles H. Brent, both of whom came to ecumenism as a result of their concern for foreign missions. Mott, the founder of the World's Student Christian Federation, devoted his entire life to bringing Christians together in service to the gospel. Brent, who worked as a missionary to non-Christians in the Philippines, became convinced that it would be, in his words, "little short of absurd to try to bring into the Church of Christ the great nations of the Far East unless we can present an undivided front. For purely practical reasons, we feel the necessity of the Church's realization of unity. It must be either that, or the failure of our vocation."[1]

Assisted by several wealthy and influential Episcopalians, Brent was the guiding force in the preparations for the First World Conference on Faith and Order, held at Lausanne in 1927. The Faith and Order movement later merged with the Life and Work Movement, founded by the Swedish Lutheran Nathan Söderblom, to constitute the World Council of Churches in 1948. The "Call to the Churches" issued prior to the First Assembly in Amsterdam defined the tasks of the new Council as follows:

> It aspires after an expression of unity in which Christians and Christian churches, joyously aware of their oneness in Jesus Christ their Lord, and pursuing an ever fuller realization of union, shall in time of need give help and comfort to one another, and at all times inspire and exhort one another to live worthily of their common membership in the Body of Christ.[2]

The Catholic Church held aloof from the ecumenical movement until the Second Vatican Council, but then, under the guidance of Pope John XXIII, it became deeply involved. In its historic *Decree on Ecumenism*, Vatican II declared: "[Discord among Christians] openly contradicts the will of Christ, provides a stumbling block to the world, and inflicts damage on the most holy cause of proclaiming the good news to every creature" (*UR* 1).

Ever since that time, Catholic papal teaching has constantly emphasized the connection between ecumenism and missionary endeavor. Paul VI in his apostolic exhortation *Evangelii nuntiandi* emphasized "the sign of unity among all Christians as the way and instrument of evangelization. The division among Christians," he wrote, "is a serious reality which impedes the very work of Christ" (*EN* 77).

Pope John Paul II took up the same theme. In the last chapter of his encyclical on Christian unity he recalled the prayer of Jesus, on the night before he died, that his disciples might all be one "so that the world may believe that you have sent me" (John 17:21; *UUS* 98). "How indeed," he asked, "can we proclaim the Gospel of reconciliation without at the same time being committed to working for reconciliation between Christians?...When nonbelievers meet missionaries who do not agree among themselves, even though they all appeal to Christ, will they be in a position to receive the true message? Will they not think that the gospel is a cause of division, despite the fact that it is presented as the fundamental law of love?" (*UUS* 98).

In his encyclical on missionary activity, the same pope had already spoken of the divisions among Christians as obstacles to the work of evangelization. But he added that ongoing efforts to reestablish unity are a source of edification, removing certain obstacles to evangelization and encouraging Christians to collaborate and bear witness together (*RMis* 50).

The ecumenical movement, if it succeeded fully in its task, would greatly contribute to the work of missionary evangelization. But, as John Paul reminded his readers, even partial successes serve to reduce mutual antipathy and increase solidarity among Christians. Every step along the path of ecumenism may be seen as a contribution to the evangelization of the non-Christian world—a world of disbelief and false belief that is present not only in some dark and distant continents, but in our very midst.

The Meaning of Evangelization

Before we examine the ways of ecumenism in greater detail, it will be helpful to clarify the meaning of the other term in my title, *evangelization*. Paul VI declares: "For the Church, evangelizing means bringing the Good News into all the strata of humanity, and through its influence transforming humanity from within and making it new" (*EN* 18). "The Church," he writes, "...exists in order to evangelize, that is to say, in order to preach and teach, to be the channel of the gift of grace, to reconcile sinners with God, and to perpetuate Christ's sacrifice in the Mass, which is the memorial of his death and glorious Resurrection" (*EN* 14). The Church as an evangelizer, he added, "begins by being evangelized herself" (*EN* 15). Evangelization, therefore, is a continuing process throughout the life of faith.

In his encyclical on missionary activity, John Paul II, building on this broad concept of evangelization, distinguished three spheres (*RMis* 33–34). The first, corresponding to the *missio ad gentes* or first evangelization, is directed to peoples who do not yet believe in Christ. The second sphere, reevangelization, is aimed at rekindling Christian faith in regions where the gospel has taken root but where the people have lost a living sense of the faith, so that they need to be converted to Christ once more. The third sphere, pastoral care, is the deeper insertion of the gospel in the hearts and minds of faithful Christians, so that they will be able to think, feel, speak, and act in full accordance with the mind of Christ. Such pastoral care falls within the comprehensive idea of evangelization set forth by Paul VI. It would be a mistake to try to draw a sharp line of division between evangelization and pastoral care.

With this introduction, we may consider the various kinds of ecumenical activity and see how each of them is related to evangelization. On the basis of Vatican II's *Decree on Ecumenism* and the encyclical of John Paul II on that subject, I believe that we may conveniently distinguish four main types of activity, which I shall treat in an order convenient for the purposes of this chapter.

Spiritual Ecumenism

The heart of the ecumenical effort, according to Vatican II, consists in spiritual ecumenism. The Council introduces this topic by stating: "There can be no ecumenism worthy of the name without a change of heart" (*UR* 7). The decree goes on to say: "The more purely they [Christ's faithful] strive to live according to the gospel, the more they are fostering and even practicing Christian unity" (*UR* 7). By deepening their communion with the triune God, they are growing in union with one another. The soul of the whole ecumenical movement therefore consists in a change of heart and holiness of life, together with public and private prayer for unity (*UR* 8).

Pope John Paul taught much the same. Interior conversion, he maintained, is essential for the renewal of the Church, without which Christian unity will never be possible (*UUS* 15). Love intensifies the desire for unity: "If we love one another, we strive to deepen our communion and make it perfect" (*UUS* 21). Love, therefore, is the undercurrent that gives vigor to the movement toward unity (ibid.).

Spiritual ecumenism also involves the virtues of humility and repentance. Even if we have sinned gravely against unity, reconciliation is still possible if we are humbly conscious of our offenses and our need for conversion (*UUS* 34). Rather than turning our minds inward upon ourselves, we should be raising them toward God, imploring his mercy and forgiveness. As Christians do this, even in their own separated communities, they will find themselves drawn together in mutual respect and love. Spiritual ecumenism requires us to be Christlike, gentle, humble, and self-denying.

Among the means whereby we draw near to Christ and receive a share in his divine life are prayer and worship, both of which must therefore be considered under the rubric of spiritual ecumenism. We can and should pray for one another, but prayer together has added efficacy. Prayers in common, says the *Decree on Ecumenism*, are a very effective means of petitioning for the grace of unity (*UR* 8). John Paul II agrees when he writes: "Along the ecumenical path toward unity, pride of place certainly belongs to common prayer, the prayerful union of those who gather together around Christ" (*UUS* 22).

Similar principles apply to worship and liturgy. Divine worship may be conducted by individuals and churches in separation, but it may sometimes be appropriate to conduct these services jointly with other communions, thereby manifesting the degree of unity in Christ that already exists.

Baptism by its very nature is a bond of unity, since it brings its recipients into the very body of Christ, making them in a sense members of one another. All the baptized share in Christ a certain mystical unity, which is of immense ecumenical importance. The other sacraments sustain and intensify this basic unity.

The Eucharist is par excellence the sacrament of ecclesiastical unity. All who worthily receive the one body of Christ become one body. The faithful who offer the Holy Sacrifice and receive Holy Communion at the same altar are brought into deeper communion with the Holy Trinity and with one another (*UR* 15). In the present situation, it is not possible for us to celebrate the Eucharist in common with churches that have not retained the fullness of the apostolic faith and ministry, but even so, the Eucharist can serve to stimulate the aspiration for unity. As John Paul II puts it in his encyclical on ecumenism: "Yet we do have a burning desire to join in celebrating the one Eucharist of the Lord, and this desire is already a common prayer of praise, a single supplication. Together we speak to the Father and increasingly we do so 'with one heart.'" (*UUS* 45; cf. *EE* 44).

The practice of spiritual ecumenism, I believe, is highly favorable to evangelization. In dealing with Jews, Muslims, and others, Christians will do well to clear the ground by honestly acknowledging the mistakes of the past that have poisoned our relations with these great faiths. Pope John Paul II did not hesitate to make apologies for the prejudices and violence that have existed in the past and in some cases continue to exist today.

Prayer, likewise, is an essential accompaniment of missionary activity. Vatican II, in its *Decree on the Church's Missionary Activity*, taught that the missionary should be a person of prayer, "imbued with a loving faith and a hope that never fails." In the spirit of sacrifice, the missionary "should bear about in himself the dying of Jesus, so that the life of Jesus may work in those to whom he is sent." He must be joined with Christ in obedience to the will of the Father (*AG* 25).

John Paul II relied heavily upon prayer as a means of overcoming the obstacles to the unity and peace that Christ seeks to bring to all peoples. "Wherever people are praying in the world," he wrote, "there the Holy Spirit is, the living breath of prayer." At his days of prayer for peace in Assisi in 1986 and 1999 he brought together leaders from many churches and from many religions. The dynamism of the Holy Spirit undergirds the efforts to overcome divisions not only within Christianity but between Christianity and other faiths. The spiritual contacts among world religions may therefore be seen as a wider form of ecumenism.

Paul VI, in his great apostolic exhortation, memorably declared that "the first means of evangelization is the witness of an authentically Christian life, given over to God in a communion that nothing should destroy and at the same time given to one's neighbor with limitless zeal" (*EN* 41). Those who evangelize, like those who engage in ecumenism, must exhibit living fidelity to the

Lord Jesus through their poverty and detachment, their freedom in the face of the powers of this world, or in short, through the witness of sanctity (ibid.). Unless Christians take seriously their responsibility to live according to the way of Christ, their efforts at ecumenism and evangelization will not succeed.

Pope John Paul II, following in the footsteps of Paul VI, frequently insisted that "the witness of the Christian life is the first and irreplaceable form of evangelization" (*RMis* 43). He went so far as to state that the true missionary is the saint (*RMis* 90). Animated by the charity of Christ, the missionary must aim "to gather into one the children of God who are scattered abroad" (John 11:52; *RMis* 89). As a sign of Christ's love in the world, the evangelizer must practice love without exclusion or partiality (*RMis* 89). The good evangelist, therefore, must have the same spiritual gifts that make for success in ecumenism.

Cooperation

The second area of ecumenism is that of collaborative action. Christians are called to show mercy upon all who are in suffering or in need. Individual Christians do so, but their efforts are reinforced when they unite in collaborative action across denominational lines. There is hardly a country in the world in which the Catholic Church is not cooperating with other Christians in working for social justice, human rights, development, and relief for the needy. In cases of natural disasters, such as floods and earthquakes, Christians of different traditions find ways of uniting for common action.

Cooperation among Christians for social causes draws them closer to one another in mutual love and respect, thus preparing the paths of unity. Such cooperation is also a way of showing the beneficial effects of the Christian faith, which calls for mercy and beneficence. Common Christian witness in works of charity, according to Vatican II, "sets in clearer relief the features of Christ the Servant" (*UR* 12). As a powerful way of bearing witness to Christ and the Gospel, it makes a distinct contribution to evangelization.

It is also possible for Christians to develop more cordial relationships with non-Christians by collaborating with them in efforts aimed at peace, international justice, and care for the environment. These efforts can overcome hostility and make non-Christians more receptive to the truths and values of the gospel. They too may be reckoned as a form of the "wider ecumenism."

Witness

The witness borne to Christ by works of charity is only indirect, since these works are primarily ordered to achieving certain social effects. But Christian witness can also be a means of proclaiming the faith and inviting others to share it. Such common witness is the third major area of ecumenism. Vatican II acknowledges the importance of such manifestations. It notes that Christians, notwithstanding their doctrinal differences, share in common some of the most important and fundamental doctrines, such as the Trinity and the Incarnation. Then it adds: "Before the whole world, let all Christians profess their faith in God, one and three, and in the incarnate Son of God, our Redeemer and Lord" (*UR* 12). In his first encyclical, *Redemptor hominis*, Pope John Paul II said that though the path to unity is long and difficult, we Christians "can and must immediately reach and display to the world our unity in proclaiming the mystery of Christ" (*RH* 11).

The supreme act of witness is usually taken to be martyrdom. The *Decree on Ecumenism* spoke of Christians who are not Catholics "bearing witness of Christ, sometimes even to the shedding of their blood" (*UR* 4). Pope John Paul II spoke of the twentieth century as being a time of great witness. At a ceremony in the Colosseum of Rome on May 7, 2000, to which representatives of other churches and ecclesial communities were invited, he commemorated the witnesses to the faith of the twentieth century. The martyrs, he contends, are "the most authentic witnesses to the truth about existence."

> From the moment they speak to us of what we perceive deep down as the truth we have sought for so long, the martyrs provide evidence of a love that has no need of lengthy arguments to convince. The martyrs stir in us a

profound trust because they give voice to what we already feel, and they declare what we would like to have the strength to express. (*FR* 32)

Sometimes, as in the case of the young men slain for the faith in Uganda, Catholics and Anglican Christians have been martyred together, giving common testimony to the saving power of Christ and the gospel "shining through our human weakness" (Preface for the Mass of Martyrs). The willingness of Christians of different communions to die for their faith in Christ is an eloquent sign of the transforming power of the gospel.

Dialogue

We turn now to the last of my four forms of ecumenical activity. Since the first World Conference on Faith and Order at Lausanne in 1927, official dialogues have been undertaken for the sake of overcoming misunderstandings and disagreements. Vatican II in its *Decree on Ecumenism* attached great importance to "'dialogue' between competent experts from different churches and ecclesial communities" (*UR* 4; cf. 9). It called for dialogue on the meaning of the Lord's Supper, the other sacraments, and the Church's worship and ministry (*UR* 22). In several places, the Council also called for dialogue with non-Christian religions (*AG* 16; *NA* 2). The *Pastoral Constitution on the Church in the Modern World* called for dialogue with nonbelievers (*GS* 92).

During the Council Paul VI published his first encyclical, *Ecclesiam suam*, encouraging dialogue in three spheres: among the entire human family, among monotheists, and among Christians. At the end of the Council, he set up secretariats for ecumenical, interreligious, and secular dialogue.

Since that time, bilateral and multilateral ecumenical conversations have led to some remarkable statements of agreement and convergence on a multitude of disputed questions. With the full participation of Catholic representatives, the Faith and Order Commission in 1982 published a highly promising paper, "Baptism, Eucharist, and Ministry." Dialogues with Jews, Muslims,

Buddhists, and Hindus have also been productive in various degrees.

John Paul II strongly supported dialogues on all levels as consonant with "today's personalist way of thinking." Dialogue, he asserted, is "an indispensable step towards human self-realization" (*UUS* 28).

It might be imagined that theological dialogues have nothing to do with evangelization because they are not directly aimed at converting the other party. In the common view, dialogue is supposed to be a nonintrusive effort to achieve reconciliation without putting any pressure on either party to change its positions. Understood in this way, it would limit itself to clearing up misunderstandings and finding common ground, so that the parties could live together more amicably.

Ecumenical dialogues differ from missionary evangelization because they are, so to speak, intramural and because they are not aimed to convert the participants to a new ecclesial allegiance. But it would be excessive to think that they are intended to leave the participants unchanged. The parties are expected to challenge one another by giving grounds for their own distinctive doctrines.

In his missionary encyclical, John Paul II cautions against false irenicism in the concept of dialogue. He warns that those engaged in the dialogues must be consistent with their own religious convictions and traditions, so that witness is given and received "for mutual advancement on the road of religious inquiry and experience" (*RMis* 56). In other documents, he applies the same principles to ecumenical dialogue. Speaking to the Roman Curia, on June 28, 1980, he declared that "the unity of Christians cannot be sought in a 'compromise' between the various theological positions, but only in the most ample and mature fullness of Christian truth."[3] When he discusses ecumenical dialogue in *Ut unum sint*, the pope proposes that "at the stage we have now reached, this process of mutual enrichment must be taken seriously into account," impelling the participating Churches toward full and visible communion (*UUS* 87).

In these texts, the pope is clearly repudiating a reductive type of interreligious dialogue or ecumenism that would bracket the distinctive tenets of each participating community and emphasize only the points of agreement. Religions and churches must ask themselves: How much can we contribute to, and receive from, one another, growing into the fullness of revealed truth? To achieve this result, the dialogue must include an element of testimony.

If we return now to the concept of evangelization that is current in official teaching, we can see that ecumenical dialogue contains within itself an ingredient of evangelization. The parties "evangelize" one another to the extent that they help one another to overcome their deficiencies and to accept authentic Christian elements that they had overlooked or neglected. Ecumenical dialogue, so understood, is not primary evangelization but is pertinent to the kind of continuing evangelization that has been advocated by recent popes.

You might ask how such mutual enrichment will affect the processes of interreligious dialogue and missionary evangelization. That question lies beyond the scope of the present chapter. I suspect that the more robust and unified Christians can be in their witness, the more successfully will they engage the interest of non-Christians. In their encounters with non-Christians they should not be complacent about themselves or truculent toward others, but in all humility they should be able to bear witness to the wonderful works of God, who has not spared his beloved Son in bringing about our redemption.

Notes

1. See Ruth Rouse and Stephen C. Neill, *A History of the Ecumenical Movement 1517–1948* (Philadelphia: Westminster, 1954), 426.

2. Ibid., 719.

3. John Paul II, Address to the Roman Curia, June 28, 1980, 17; in his *Addresses and Homilies on Ecumenism 1978–1980* (Washington, DC: United States Catholic Conference, 1981), 126–30, at 130.

Chapter 6

The Evangelization of Culture and the Catholic University

The Catholic university, as a matter of its essential character, can be said to exist to serve a purpose that can be described as "the evangelization of culture." Discovering, more precisely, what this purpose means and what this role for the Catholic university entails calls for a closer exploration of the connections among three realities: culture, evangelization, and the Catholic university. Recognizing that the three are closely interrelated, John Paul II, in his Apostolic Constitution on Catholic Universities, *Ex corde Ecclesiae*, devotes the last two chapters respectively to "Cultural Dialogue" and "Evangelization."[1] The term *evangelization of culture*, which appears in my title, was first used by Paul VI in his apostolic exhortation *Evangelii nuntiandi.*[2] Frequently echoed by John Paul II, the term has by now passed into general usage.

The Idea of Culture

Let me begin with some reflections on the idea of culture. In its broadest meaning, this idea embraces everything that human beings do to refashion themselves and the world in which they live. Culture is the realm of reason, freedom, and creativity; it is the sphere of truth, beauty, and goodness. Spiritual in its source and finality, culture takes root in the physical world: it becomes incarnate, so to speak, in visible and palpable symbols, which express and communicate interior attitudes.

Normally, also, the term *culture* has a social connotation: it is used to designate the world in which people share through their insertion into communities. In its full extent, culture includes all the customs and institutions that serve to make life more human. In a more specialized sense, it refers to the exceptional achievements of thought, art, and literature by which people express their loftiest spiritual experiences and insights. Different ethnic and social entities develop their own distinctive cultures, which must be respected both in education and in the ministry of the Church.[3]

Culture is also closely linked with history. The achievements of one age are handed down to the next in a process known as tradition. Without tradition, society would be in a situation like that of an individual deprived of memory. It would continually find itself faced with the necessity of beginning again from the most primitive stage.

Every culture carries with it a particular set of traditions, values, and convictions. Different cultures embody the ethnic and historical traits of particular peoples. Not all cultures are equally good; none can claim to be perfect. Because human beings are subject to sin and error, culture can be distorted or perverse. It can glorify evils such as cannibalism, infant sacrifice, and temple prostitution. Rudimentary cultures need to be strengthened and enriched; decadent cultures need to be purified and regenerated; advanced cultures need to be perfected and harnessed to address the needs and problems of particular times and places.

From these preliminary observations, it should be obvious that culture is closely linked with education. Education could almost be defined as the process of socializing students into the culture or some aspect of it, so that they may rise above merely material concerns, profit from the achievements of their forebears, live in communion with their fellows, pass on what they have received, and perhaps contribute to further progress. Education takes place initially in the family and the neighborhood; it is fostered by multiple means of communication, including news media, music, and the arts. But education is most formally conducted in schools, and at its highest levels, in universities and graduate schools. University graduates are expected to be men and women of more than ordinary culture.

Christ and Culture

The relationships between Christ and culture have been variously understood. Christ is proclaimed in Holy Scripture and in the teaching of the Church as the way, the truth, and the life (John 14:6). In his incarnate life, he encounters human culture. In many respects he shares in the culture of late Judaism. Using the languages of his time and place, he interprets his mission in terms of the Scriptures, religious practices, and customs of the people into which he was born, even while importing new wine that would inevitably burst the wineskins of ancient Judaism (Matt 9:17).

In some respects, the encounter is hostile: Christ stands against the culture and it against him. He condemns all that is sinful and self-centered and in so doing provokes antipathy. Christianity calls for a cultural revolution more radical than that which Mao Tse-tung sought to achieve in China during the twentieth century. Without violently displacing the cultures that receive it, Christianity acts as a ferment in the culture, incessantly seeking to achieve what Friedrich Nietzsche, in another context, called a "transvaluation of all values."[4]

Depending on their respective capacities, different human cultures are capable of receiving Christ and his gospel in different modes and measures. Standing above all cultures as their Lord, Christ aims to transform and enrich them. To the extent that human culture opens its doors to his holy influence, he heals, ennobles, and perfects it (*RMis* 54). But humanity, marked as it is by finitude and sin, never fully receives all that Christ has to offer: It continually puts up resistance. He and they are dialectically interrelated. Christ and culture are therefore in unceasing tension.

We sometimes speak of Christian or Catholic cultures. To the extent that individuals and communities sincerely subject themselves to Christ, they are able to create cultures that reflect and inculcate the truths and values of the gospel. Christ, filled with the truth and goodness of the divinity, is an unfailing source of wisdom and virtue. He manifests the being and purposes of God, and in so doing, as Vatican II reminds us, he reveals the meaning of creation and of human existence. We understand ourselves more accurately in terms of what he teaches about the sources, norms, and goals of our existence. In him, the riddles of suffering and death become meaningful (*GS* 22). If humanity as a whole were to follow his teaching and example, it would be able to achieve on earth a culture of peace and solidarity, a civilization of love. But where society refuses the help of its divine Redeemer, it inevitably condemns itself to decline and dissolution. It generates what John Paul II characterized as an anticulture of hatred and violence.[5]

The Transmission of Christian Culture

Gradually in the course of his earthly career, and especially in his risen life, Christ constituted the Church and equipped her to carry on his work under the direction of his Spirit. In particular, he entrusted the Church with his message for the world, a message that may be briefly referred to as the gospel. The transmission of the gospel is an event of the supernatural order, depending on the lively assistance of the Holy Spirit. The Church, sent to the farthest corners of the globe, has no deeper desire than to offer Christ the King the riches of all the nations as an inheritance (*LG* 13).

The Church, then, has a message vital for the redemption of individual persons and of society as a whole. She proclaims her message by announcing the basic Christian *kerygma*, by catechesis, by liturgical preaching, by her creeds and doctrines, by the example of saintly lives. Drawing on the true insights and sound methods of secular cultures, the Church seeks to infuse them with the higher values of the gospel. Christianity has been a mighty formative influence on certain cultures such as the medieval cultures of Byzantium and western Europe. Faith, impregnating the heritage of Greco-Roman antiquity and igniting the genius of new native populations, gave rise to a brilliant flourishing of philosophy, literature, art, and music.

Christian educational institutions play a vital role in the genesis, development, and transmission of Christian culture. The Church uses them as instruments in the Christianization of the world. With their help, she transmits her literary, artistic, political, and philosophical heritage to new generations. Christian education forms believers capable of preserving, disseminating, and enriching that healthy and salutary culture to the benefit of the secular world itself.

Evangelization and Culture

In speaking of the cultural influence of the Church, I am already touching on the second theme of this chapter, evangelization. Because of its complexity, this notion is frequently misunderstood. In the narrowest sense, it refers to the proclamation of the gospel to those who do not yet believe. But this activity, sometimes called "first evangelization," is only one stage of a larger process. Prior to conversion, people can often be prepared to hear the word by a process known as preevangelization, and after conversion they are expected to submit to continued evangelization in order to achieve Christian maturity. At times, having fallen away from the gospel, Christians are in need of reevangelization. Evangelization in its full sense of the word includes all three stages: the announcement of the gospel to those who have not yet heard it credibly proclaimed, the pastoral care and religious maturation of believers, and the rekindling of faith in those who have fallen away.

The word *evangelization* is applied in an analogous sense to cultures. Cultures themselves do not believe or disbelieve, but they can contain elements that are in conformity with the Christian message or opposed to it. To evangelize a culture is to purify and transform it in light of the gospel so that it reflects authentic Christian values and becomes a suitable vehicle for the evangelization of persons individually and in groups.

Evangelization and Higher Education

The university has a real but limited role with respect to evangelization. Not being a church, the university cannot be expected to bear the full burden of evangelization. It is by definition a place concerned with the pursuit of knowledge, and more specifically with the kind of knowledge that can be suitably transmitted in an academic setting. The university educates by teaching facts, forming theories to interpret the facts, and appraising such theories by critical thought and experimentation. Unlike preaching, academic instruction is not directly aimed at eliciting acts of faith. Faith, desirable though it may be in university students, is not proper material for examination and academic grading. A sound education in conformity with Christian principles can help individuals to receive the faith and grow in it.

Since the Enlightenment, a very influential school of thinkers has contended that universities must by definition be secular.[6] Secular knowledge, according to these scholars, is accessible to all normal human beings through the exercise of their rational faculties; it relies upon no supernatural graces or freely chosen options. Secular knowledge is in that sense public. Religion, these thinkers assert, is something that takes place in intimate relations between the individual soul and its God; it is a matter of the heart more than the mind. Religion can of course be studied as a human phenomenon in courses on philosophy, psychology, and sociology, all of which employ secular methodologies; but the study of God as apprehended in faith, according to this school of thought, does not belong in the university. For this reason, the secularist tradition maintains, Christian theology should be ejected from the university and confined to seminaries and divinity schools that operate under ecclesiastical auspices.

This line of reasoning, obviously, makes nonsense of the idea of a Christian or Catholic university. It is based on a theology that is Lutheran or, more accurately, ultra-Lutheran. It presupposes the position of Immanuel Kant, according to which faith and knowledge are mutually exclusive. Faith, in this view, is an act of the will or practical reason that enters in only at the point where verifiable knowledge reaches its limit.

The statutes of the University of Berlin in the early nineteenth century were drawn up under the influence of Lutheran theologians such as Friedrich Schleiermacher. Many universities, following this trend, excluded theology from the university curriculum on the ground that it did not satisfy the Kantian criteria of genuine knowledge. They treated theology as a practical science pertaining to the professional training of ministers of religion.[7]

This secularist mentality has more than a little to do with the drift of most of the universities founded under Protestant and Anglican auspices from their Christian roots during the nineteenth and early twentieth centuries. The majority of universities in the United States today buy into what we may call the Berlin model.[8]

They allow for "religious studies" but not theology as a confessional discipline. In the Catholic view, which is shared by some Christians of other communities, no such separation between faith and knowledge is acceptable. Faith does not begin where reason ends but, on the contrary, brings reason to its highest fulfillment by providing the added light of revelation. Since God is truth, revelation conveys true knowledge and is no less certain than any secular science.

Revelation, moreover, is public inasmuch as it is destined for the whole of humankind. As the Alpha and Omega of the universe, Christ is essential not just for the Church and its members but for the entire human project. Without the help of revelation, reason would be unable to attain its connatural objective; it would fall short of the wisdom to which it aspires. Without obedience to the word of God, humanity would strive in vain for a universal civilization of peace and love.

The Contemporary Situation

Since the rise of universities in western Europe in the Middle Ages—until the nineteenth century—most universities were institutionally committed to the truth of Christian revelation. In Catholic and Protestant universities alike, the theology faculty was accorded the highest place of honor. The Harvard College Laws of 1642, for example, affirmed Christ as the foundation of all knowledge and learning, stating that "Every one shall consider the mayne end of his life and studyes to know God and Jesus Christ which is Eternall life....Seeing the Lord giveth wisdome, every one shall seriously by prayer in secret, seeketh wisdome of him."[9]

John Henry Newman, in the mid–nineteenth century, spoke in similar terms in his *The Idea of a University*. Since God is the Supreme Being, he argued, and since much can be known about God from reason and revelation, any university that leaves out the study of theology is gravely defective.[10]

Degrees in theology have traditionally been conferred by ecclesiastical officeholders known as chancellors, as they are at The Catholic University of America today. At a time when theologians normally held ecclesiastical degrees from Catholic faculties and taught with ecclesiastical approval, theological faculties exercised a certain magisterial role in the Church. They were frequently consulted on the orthodoxy of controversial theological opinions. The opinions of Luther, for example, were evaluated by a succession of universities before the pope condemned his teachings.[11] Recognizing the Church as the authoritative bearer of revelation, Catholic theology faculties, today as in the past, cooperate closely with popes and bishops, though in less formal ways than before the Reformation.

Catholic universities in the United States do not always measure up to the ideal. Under the influence of the prevailing secular culture, some have drifted far in the direction of what I have called the Berlin model. A number have done away with theology entirely, admitting only "religious studies," considered as an essentially secular discipline that accords no normative status to Christian or Catholic doctrine. In other cases theology itself, while it survives by name, is taught from a religiously uncommitted point of view and is scarcely distinguishable from a sociological or historical study of religion.

Under John Paul II and Benedict XVI, some of the lost territory has been reclaimed. Theology is once again being recognized as a sacred discipline inseparable from faith and from the Church as the authorized bearer of faith. Efforts are being made to reconstitute ecclesiastical faculties in Catholic universities throughout the world and to see to it that Catholic universities without ecclesiastical faculties teach theology in harmony with the doctrine of the Church.

Catholic universities, while giving due emphasis to theology, must also cultivate many other disciplines. They should teach the traditional arts and sciences and give professional preparation in certain specialties such as law, medicine, and education. In countries such as the United States, much of the humanistic formation given by the *lycée* or the *gymnasium* in Europe has become the responsibility of colleges and universities. This enables universities to take on a greater role in the formation and transmission of culture. Catholic universities can be powerful instruments for the maintenance and development of Catholic culture.

In the American system, the threat of secularism has been compounded with the disease of fragmentation. Departmentalism aggravates the academic chaos of what some call "multiversities." Even Catholic universities have been plagued by the internecine rivalry of departments struggling for territory and independence. But the manifest deficiencies of this situation provide an occasion for Catholic universities to show a better way.

John Paul II dwelt on this possibility in his apostolic constitution, *Ex corde Ecclesiae*. He writes:

> A University and especially a Catholic university, *has to be a 'living union' of individual organisms* dedicated to the search for truth....It is necessary *to work towards a higher synthesis* of knowledge, in which alone lies the possibility of satisfying that thirst for truth which is profoundly inscribed on the heart of the human person." Aided by the specific contributions of philosophy and theology, university scholars will be engaged in a constant effort to determine the relative place and meaning of each of the various disciplines within the context of a vision of the human person and the world that is enlightened by the gospel, and therefore by a faith in Christ, the *Logos*, as the centre of creation and of human history.[12]

In modern times, theology has become rather self-enclosed as the study of what is strictly deducible from the revealed word of God. In most cases, it lacks the breadth of vision reflected in the writings of an Augustine or an Aquinas. Vatican II hints at a broader and more sapiential concept, recalling that faith casts a new light on reality as a whole (*GS* 11). In the setting of a Catholic university, the arts and sciences will be taught from the perspective of faith and therefore in close relationship with theology.

Philosophy, for example, will recognize that it is dealing with many of the ultimate questions that are studied from a different perspective in theology—questions such as the existence and nature of God, the creation of contingent beings, the dignity of the human person, the immortality of the soul, the relationship between soul and body, and innumerable other questions of this kind. Professors of philosophy, recognizing the limits of their method, will not try to answer specifically theological questions, but they will indicate how their conclusions cohere with a generally Christian and Catholic worldview, thus contributing to what I like to call integral Christian wisdom.

A similar interpenetration with faith occurs in many other disciplines. I can only suggest the immensity of the possibilities by adducing a few examples. Psychology in a Catholic university will base itself on a sound Christian anthropology, not on the atheistic presuppositions of Sigmund Freud or the Gnostic religiosity of Carl Jung. Social science and economics will avoid the utilitarianism of Jeremy Bentham and the materialistic determinism of Karl Marx. Political science will be taught with close attention to the dignity of the individual person and the common good. Courses in literature will probe the religious message conveyed by poets such as Chaucer and Dante or by novelists such as Alessandro Manzoni and Sigrid Undset, Evelyn Waugh and Graham Greene. The study of music will not shy away from exploring the dimension of worship found in Gregorian chant, in the polyphony of Palestrina, and the oratorios of Bach. In the study of art, religious themes will not be obscured by exclusive attention to merely formalistic considerations. Courses on journalism, communications, and the information sciences will advert to the ethical dimensions of these arts and their value as vehicles for the transmission of religious truth. Professional studies in fields such as medicine and law need not be taught with an exclusive view to success in a career. Seen rather as vocations to service, these fields should be studied with a distinctively Christian and Catholic emphasis. Medicine will not ignore the serious human problems raised by biotechnology and genetic engineering. Jurisprudence will situate itself in the tradition of Francisco de Vitoria, Francisco Suárez, and Juan de Lugo. Legal ethics will take cognizance of contemporary Catholic social teaching.

In the measure that faith is still vibrant within them, Catholic universities are in a privileged position to appropriate the great achievements of the Judeo-Christian tradition. But the focus should not be exclusively on the past. It is not too much to hope that such universities may foster creativity in the Catholic tradition. John Paul II indicated as much. In a dialogue with His Holiness at Los Angeles in 1987, Archbishop Rembert Weakland declared that the Church of the United States could "boast of having the largest number of educated faithful in the world." The pope replied that in that case the Church should be in a position to exercise great influence on American culture. And then the pope asked:

> But how is the American culture evolving today? Is this evolution being influenced by the gospel? Does it clearly reflect a Christian inspiration? Your music, your poetry and art, your drama, your painting and sculpture, the literature that you are producing—are all those things which reflect the soul of a nation being influenced by the spirit of Christ for the perfection of humanity?[13]

One test of the effectiveness of Catholic education might be the behavior of its graduates. Do Catholic politicians, for example, stand up for Christian principles rather than mere expediency? Do Catholic parents stay united and bring up Christian families? Do Catholics in business set an example of integrity? I am afraid that we would find all too many failures.

I am aware of the danger of excessive insularity. Vatican II sought to escape this introversion by insisting on a two-way interaction with the modern world. In the contemporary situation it is necessary for Catholic intellectuals to take account of the variety of religions and enter into respectful dialogue with them as well as with secular sciences. Religious studies, conducted according to Catholic principles, will prove particularly useful in building bridges across religious and ideological divides and contributing to an environment of mutual respect, friendship, and cooperation.

Concluding Reflections

Not all Catholic universities have the same relationship to the Church. Some are established and governed by the Holy See or the bishops. Others, more tenuously related to the hierarchical leadership, may understandably make less of their Catholic identity and seek to accommodate faculty and students of many different persuasions. But all are institutional, committed to the truth of the

Catholic faith and are subject to the norms of the apostolic constitution *Ex corde Ecclesiae*.

I do not mean to urge an obsessive preoccupation with being distinctively Catholic, as though Catholic identity had to be defined against everything else. On the contrary, the Catholic tendency is to be inclusive, welcoming whatever is good and true in every human culture. Nor am I advocating a rigid conformism in which obedience to hierarchical teaching would be accepted as a substitute for rigorous scholarly reflection. The university must be a place of serious research in which genuine questions are asked and answered. It must be solicitous to preserve academic freedom, rightly understood. Precisely in order to serve the Church, the university must jealously protect the rightful freedom of scholars in the Church to use the methodologies of their particular disciplines. According to the medieval maxim *"non ancilla nisi libera,"*[14] the university would not be able to be truly helpful to the Church if it were not free in its own order.

My strongest recommendation is for Catholic universities to make all their departments transmitters and builders of Catholic culture. Culture is not a mere epiphenomenon tossed about by the stronger forces of politics, economics, and military might. My reading of history convinces me of the opposite. As George Weigel has written:

> The deepest currents of history are spiritual and cultural, rather than political and economic....History is driven, over the long haul, by culture—by what men and women honor, cherish, and worship; by what societies deem to be true and good, and by the expressions they give to those convictions in language, literature, and the arts; by what individuals and societies are willing to stake their lives on.[15]

The United States is today in danger of succumbing to the culture of secularization that has all but won the day in western Europe. As Christopher Dawson saw with prophetic clarity, the culture of the West cannot survive apart without keeping its religious tradition alive.[16] In countering this tendency Catholic universities can play a crucial role.

Notes

1. Pope John Paul II, apostolic constitution *Ex corde Ecclesia* §§43–47; *Origins* 20 (October 4, 1990), 265–76.

2. Pope Paul VI, apostolic exhortation *Evangelii nuntiandi*, §20 (Washington, DC: United States Catholic Conference, 1976), 16–17.

3. In this paragraph, I am essentially following the ideas of John Paul II. Some of his more important writings on the subject are reprinted in *The Church and Culture Since Vatican II: The Experience of North and Latin America*, ed. Joseph Gremillion (Notre Dame, IN: University of Notre Dame Press, 1985). I have discussed these and other texts in Avery Dulles, *The Splendor of Faith: The Theological Vision of Pope John Paul II*, 153–69 (New York: Crossroad, rev. & updated ed., 2003).

4. Friedrich Nietzsche, "The AntiChrist: An Essay Towards a Criticism of Christianity" (1896), reprinted in *Twilight of the Idols and the Antichrist*, trans. Thomas Common, (Mineola, NY: Dover Publications, 2004), 84.

5. Pope John Paul II, Address to the Second Annual Meeting of the Pontifical Council for Culture (Jan. 16, 1984), reprinted in Gremillion, *The Church and Culture Since Vatican II*, 207–9.

6. This movement originated in Germany during the Enlightenment. For discussion see Friedrich Paulsen, *The German Universities and University Study* (New York: Scribner, 1906); Daniel Fallon, *The German University: A Heroic Ideal in Conflict with the Modern World* (Boulder, CO: Colorado Assoicated University Press, 1980).

7. David H. Kelsey, in his *To Understand God Truly: What's Theological About a Theological School* (Louisville, KY.: Westminster/ John Knox Press, 1992), observes that Schleiermacher's "rationale for including theology *as a professional school* in the research university has deeply shaped theological schooling in twentieth-century North America, especially in the United States," 92.

8. George M. Marsden, in works such as *The Soul of the American University: From Protestant Establishment to Established Nonbelief* (New York: Oxford University Press, 1994), gives much information regarding the status of theology in American universities.

9. Laws and Statutes for Students of Harvard College, Harvard College Lawes of 1642, *New England's First Fruits* (London: Henry Overton, 1643), 22.

10. John Henry Newman, Discourse II, "Theology as a Branch of Knowledge," *The Idea of a University*, ed. Ian Ker (Oxford: Oxford University Press, 1976), 31–50.

11. When Luther posted his *Ninety-five Theses*, he also sent a copy to the local archbishop, who then sent them to the faculty at the University of Mainz for evaluation. Additionally, Johann Eck, a professor at the University of Ingoldstadt, closely examined the theses at the request of the Bishop of Eichstätt. Before issuing the bull *Exsurge* condemning Luther's doctrine, the Holy See obtained opinions from three committees and made use of the judgments of several university faculties, including those of the universities of Cologne and Louvain, submitted in 1519. See Erwin Iserloh, "Martin Luther and the Coming of the Reformation (1517–1525)" in *History of the Church*, vol. 5 *Reformation and Counter Reformation*, eds. Hubert Jedin and John Dolan (New York: Seabury Press, 1980), 72. The theological faculty of the University of Paris later reviewed and condemned Luther's teachings.

12. *Ex corde Ecclesiae*, §16.

13. John Paul II, "U.S. Pilgrimage: Los Angeles Meeting of the Pope and U.S. Bishops, *Origins* 17 (October 1, 1987): 263.

14. "In order to serve one must be free."

15. George Weigel, "Europe's Problem—and Ours," *First Things* No. 140 (February 2004), 18–25, at 21.

16. Christopher Dawson powerfully expressed the need for religion to provide the power to offset the cold inhumanity and the scientific exploitation of evil manifest in the new paganism in his *The Judgment of the Nations* (New York: Sheed & Ward, 1942), 221–22.

Chapter 7

The New Evangelization and Theological Renewal

Evangelization is not and never has been easy. Today we tend to blame the prevalent culture for our lack of success. We denounce its individualism, secularism, relativism, hedonism, and other vices, which do indeed render the environment unfriendly to the proclamation of the gospel. But we too easily overlook the deep religious hunger that continues to stir in the hearts of contemporary men and women. Discontented with a civilization of gadgets and entertainment, many are looking for some overarching meaning in life. For all its worldliness, the United States remains a remarkably religious nation—a nation, as G. K. Chesterton once said, with the soul of a church. Many evangelically oriented sects and churches—Mormons, Adventists, Pentecostals, and Southern Baptists, for example—are winning enormous numbers of converts. One wonders why, with all the official encouragement given to evangelization by Vatican II and the recent popes, Catholics are for the most part ready to leave the task to Protestants, some of whom are overtly hostile to Catholicism.

The reluctance of Catholics to evangelize has many roots: historical, sociological, cultural, and political. In this chapter, I shall restrict my attention to the theological roots. Catholic theology, in my opinion, still lags behind the evangelical shift that has taken place on the level of the Church's pastoral leadership. The program of evangelization calls for a renewal of Catholic theology, so that it may contribute to, rather than retard, the evangelical effort.

In seeking the right principles for an evangelically oriented theology that is fully consonant with Catholic Christianity, we could not do better than to look to the New Testament. The

Gospels, the Acts, and the Letters of Paul are permeated by such a theology. The New Testament understands the Church as an expansive community, divinely commissioned to extend to all peoples the saving message of Jesus Christ. Jesus is the content and the principal bearer of the gospel. Dwelling in the hearts of those who are baptized into his body, and actively present in their preaching and testimony, he inwardly moves and assists the faithful to carry on his work. In biblical terms, the gospel may be described as the saving power of the risen Christ, exercised in and through the Church by means of word, sacrament, and personal witness.

In Jesus, person and mission are identified. His mission on earth stands in unbroken continuity with his eternal existence within the godhead. As Son, he is perfectly obedient to the Father, from whom he receives all that he is and does. Sent into the world by Christ, the Church is the gathering of those who engage themselves to travel on the road marked out by him. They seek to show that he is for all humanity, as he is for the baptized, the way, the truth, and the life. Taken up into the body of Christ and directed by the Holy Spirit, Christians become bearers of the good news by their speech, their actions, and their whole mode of being. Like Jesus himself, they have an essentially missionary existence.

Building on these biblical themes, theology seeks to show the connection between the word of God and the truth that leads to salvation. As "salutary truth," the gospel rescues believers from death and gives them a share in eternal life. Taken up into the "pro-existence" of Christ the Redeemer, the Christian feels driven to declare by word and work the wonderful deeds of God. Because faith flowers into testimony, the theology of faith is inseparable from a theology of witness. All the truths of revelation draw their meaning and power from their relationship to Christ's redemptive action, which comes to expression in the gospel, the *evangelium*.

A theology that is both Catholic and evangelical differs from medieval Scholasticism and Counter-Reformation apologetics. These theologies contained much that is true and permanently valid; they lent themselves well to the situation of earlier centuries, when

Europe was a self-contained Christian society, but are no longer adequate for the complex global culture of our day. Medieval Scholasticism was a theology for professors and graduate students, highly speculative in its orientation. Presuming the truth of revelation and the authority of the canonical sources, it pursued subtle theoretical questions with great acumen. But, as Luther and Erasmus recognized, it did not greatly help in the business of proclaiming the gospel. The apologetically oriented theology of recent centuries, although it was more practical in orientation, was too rationalistic and ecclesiocentric to be called evangelical. The primary goal of that theology was to argue unbelievers into Catholic faith and induce a docile acceptance of "whatever the Church teaches." An evangelical theology, by contrast, seeks to reflect on the ways in which the Holy Spirit transforms the gospel into the power of salvation for all who believe.

Christian faith, understood in evangelical terms, is much more than an intellectual assent. It is a complex act involving the whole person—mind, will, and emotions. In believing I entrust myself to God as he makes himself known by his word. Faith includes a cognitive element, for it could not arise unless one were intellectually convinced that God is, has spoken, and has said what we take to be his word. But in believing I entrust myself to this God and, if I am sincere, commit myself to live according to that word. An evangelically oriented theology will explore these various dimensions of faith. Evangelization is not complete with the first proclamation of the gospel. It is a lifelong process of letting the gospel permeate and transform all our ideas and attitudes. Theology itself is an exercise in the process of evangelization, for it seeks to draw out the implications of the gospel for our understanding of reality as a whole.

A truly Catholic form of evangelical theology will differ not only from earlier Catholic theologies but also from its Protestant counterparts. Unlike some Protestant evangelicalism, it will not be predicated on the doctrine of salvation by faith alone. It will seek to renew the entire life of believers, of the Church, and of society itself through the leaven of the gospel. Hence, it will not separate word from sacraments, or faith from works, or personal morality from social action. It will strive to regenerate the entire community of believers in the light of the gospel and to transform the larger secular society in the image of the kingdom of God. Catholic evangelical theology will seek to distance itself from a number of crosscurrents in contemporary Catholicism. In a laudable attempt to meet the modern mind on its own terms, Catholic theology has sometimes failed to guard sufficiently against certain deviations that inhibit a vigorous program of evangelization. Seeking to avoid the alleged triumphalism of the past, some theologians have cultivated an attitude of hypercriticism and debilitating doubt, verging on defeatism. In their efforts to recognize the failures of the Church and the truth present in other faiths, they have often tended to substitute dialogue for proclamation, and have hesitated to confront their hearers with the challenge of the gospel. In this situation, we need fresh theological initiatives that pick up those themes in the New Testament and classical theology that previously undergirded evangelization. I should like to illustrate this with reference to seven trends in contemporary Catholic theology that are less than friendly to evangelization.

The first of these trends, in my enumeration, is the radical separation sometimes made between faith and belief. Some assert that faith is not a special gift of grace but a universal human quality found in different forms in all religions and ideologies. In transcendental theology, saving faith is frequently depicted as an interior orientation toward an encompassing mystery—a mystery that is inseparable from human nature itself. We are told, for example, that faith can be found in persons of any religion, and even in those who believe that they must be atheists, provided that such persons are obedient to the demands of conscience. The impression is given that all who accept themselves unconditionally, without self-rejection, and thus fulfill their primordial capacity for the transcendent, have faith in a satisfactory measure.

Faith, in this view, can exist without any definite set of beliefs, and hence without the gospel. The implication seems to be that there is no need to proclaim the gospel in order to bring people to faith. Anyone who accepts the inbuilt orientation of the human spirit to the nameless transcendent mystery is already an "anonymous Christian," on the path of salvation. Salvation is seen as the fruit of self-acceptance rather than of obedience to an externally spoken or written word.

Indeed, one can easily find contemporary authors who deny that any specific beliefs can be matters of faith. Faith, they declare, has no object that can be expressed in propositions. All the articles of the creed and dogmas of the Church, and the gospel message itself, in their estimation, are human constructs rather than divinely revealed truths.

This thesis, I believe, is incompatible with a vigorous program of evangelization. We need to see again what seemed evident to the early Christians—that the gospel preached by the apostles and their fellow workers is the word of God, and must be received as such. Paul, for example, was able to write to the Thessalonians: "We thank God constantly for this, that when you received the word of God which you heard from us, you accepted it not as the word of man but as what it really is, the word of God, which is at work in you believers" (1 Thess 2:13).

This Pauline teaching, which is consonant with that of the other New Testament authors and the classical theological tradition, does not require one to hold that all unevangelized peoples are consigned to eternal damnation. Indeed, the Catholic Church has repeatedly proclaimed that God puts salvation within reach of everyone. But the way in which people can be saved without hearing the gospel remains God's secret. We may conjecture that they are saved by accepting seeds of the Word (*semina Verbi*), which the divine Sower has liberally disseminated throughout the world, far and wide. But these seeds of the word do not suffice for a mature and developed faith. They are mere hints of an answer yet to be given, and cry out for completion. The gospel message concerning the incarnation, death, and resurrection of Jesus Christ remains the normal path to salvation. Apart from it no one can be secure from serious error or have access to the saving truth in its fullness.

Faith, therefore, is not simply the acceptance of an inner orientation of the human spirit to some kind of absolute transcendence. As Paul put it, "Faith comes from hearing, and hearing comes from the preaching of Christ" (Rom 10:17). Unless we are convinced of the primacy of hearing, we shall not be of service in the present call for the Church to launch a new program of evangelization.

The present reluctance to proclaim the gospel is intensified by a second theological deviation. Metaphysical agnosticism, typified in the philosophy of Immanuel Kant, maintains that nothing speculatively true can be said about God, because the human mind can have assured knowledge only about phenomena—things that appear to the senses. Accepting this philosophical stance, some theologians conclude that revelation gives no genuine knowledge about God and the supernatural. Anything we say about God is taken to be a metaphor that symbolically reaches out to the encompassing mystery, which is incomprehensible and ineffable. Since metaphors are arbitrary and expendable, say these theologians, no one can be required to profess the articles of the Christian creed.

To overcome metaphysical agnosticism, which undermines the realism of faith, we need to retrieve the tried and true doctrine of analogy. When we speak of God as wise, loving, and just, or as existing in three persons, or as creating and redeeming the world, we are making statements that are literally though analogously true. These statements are not metaphorical, like the statements that God is a rock or a shield. The biblical metaphors, however, are themselves charged with cognitive value, and may not be arbitrarily discarded. Bound up as they are with the word of God, they are part of the sacred heritage that is to be proclaimed to all peoples.

Faith, of course, lacks the perfect clarity of direct vision. There is a sense, of course, in which God remains hidden from us so long as we are in this life. Because God dwells in inaccessible light (1 Tim 6:16), we know him only obscurely, as reflected in the mirror of faith (cf. 1 Cor 13:12). But, thanks to Christ and the Holy Spirit, we do know him. Faith in the biblical and Christian sense of the word has never been a mere experience of the ineffable. Paul did speak of a mystical encounter in which he was "caught up into the third heaven" and heard things that cannot be told (2 Cor 12:1–4). But this was not the gospel he proposed for the faith of his communities. Convinced of the intelligibility of the Christian message, he could write: "Even if our gospel is veiled, it is veiled only to those who are perishing. In their case the god of this world has blinded the minds of the unbelievers, to keep them from seeing the light of the gospel..." (2 Cor 4:3–4).

A third obstacle to evangelization is a kind of religious pragmatism that is rarely formulated in explicit statements but is implicit in much contemporary religious literature. Faith is esteemed not because it is true but because it leads to desirable effects, whether personal or social. We are told, for example, that faith leads to peace of mind, psychological balance, success in business, social progress, or liberation of the oppressed. In this view it makes little difference whether the God in whom one believes is a reality or a fiction. The saving effects are regarded as coming not from God but from belief itself.

The biblical authors and classical theologians would heartily agree that faith normally brings with it many psychological and social benefits. But these are not the heart of the matter. For them it is essential that faith be true, for it gets its saving power from its reliance on the only power that can effectively vanquish the destructive forces of sin and death. Faith, in other words, saves by reason of its object. If we were not convinced that salvation comes from the God who speaks his saving word in Christ, we could perhaps be good therapists or social engineers but not evangelists.

A fourth enemy of evangelization is the reigning cultural relativism. In many circles today, it is almost a dogma that no dogma can be valid cross-culturally. Since cultures are tied to their time and place, the Christian message—it is claimed—has to be radically reconstructed for every region and every generation. To proclaim the doctrines of the New Testament and the creeds is often denigrated as a form of cultural imperialism. In particular the dogmas of the ancient councils and of the Catholic Church are dismissed as sedimentations of a Greco-Roman culture that must be consigned to the ash heap of history. If the old dogmas have any value, it is to stimulate us to concoct new dogmas appropriate to our own age.

In my judgment, this cultural and historical relativism is itself behind the times. It ignores the fact that the world is becoming a global village in which ideas and attitudes travel with the speed of light. Since every idea is received according to the condition of the recipient, adaptations will inevitably occur. But truth, whether in science or religion, transcends all cultural barriers. Any true statement, properly understood, is true everywhere and always. In any great religion, such as Christianity, Judaism, Buddhism, and Islam, there will be constants, and indeed the very value of the religion depends upon its capacity to transcend the fads and fashions of the day. A totally ephemeral religion might capture momentary interest but would not long hold the allegiance of its members.

Biblical and traditional Christianity has never been bound to a particular culture. In Christ, there is no East nor West. He is to be worshiped by Jews and Gentiles, by barbarians and Greeks. He is the same yesterday, today, and forever, and his gospel is eternal.

Modern ethnology places increasing emphasis on anthropological constants, which make it possible for people to appreciate the cultural achievements of civilizations remote from their own. The writings of ancient authors such as Plato, Virgil, and Cicero are not unintelligible to modern Americans such as ourselves. Indeed, they are often more intelligible to us than the works of twentieth-century philosophers such as Whitehead, Wittgenstein, and Heidegger. For the same reason, it is easier to proclaim the gospel in the relatively simple language of the New Testament and the early creeds than in the involved rhetoric of some contemporary theologians who offer new and original confessions of faith.

What is correct in the recent approach is the recognition that the human mind formulates revealed truth in concepts and language that are historically conditioned. The manner of expression must be adapted to different audiences, as Paul recognized when he said that he became a Jew to Jews and a Greek to Greeks in order to win them to Christ (cf. 1 Cor 9:19–23). But the truth of the gospel does not change. Paul invoked an anathema on anyone who would try to preach a different gospel than that which he had received and handed on (Gal 1:8–9).

Connected with the cultural relativism of the day is a fifth deviation: religious pluralism. If truth is "polymorphic," in the sense that it varies from race to race and from age to age, it would seem that Christianity cannot be proclaimed in new times and places. In an extreme form, this relativism leads to the conclusion that every people should have its own religion. Under the rubric of "soteriological pluralism" some modern theologians deny that Jesus Christ is the Savior of the world. Each religion is said to have its own way of salvation, its own myths, and very often its own savior figures. Christians may believe in Jesus as their savior provided that they are ready to allow other races to worship other savior figures, such as the Lord Krishna and the Lord Buddha. The saving power of any such figure is thought to consist in its mythic impact on the psyche of the believer rather than the actual mediation of the person believed in.

This soteriological pluralism, which is patently antithetical to any program of evangelization, can seem very appealing in an age when we are reacting against the so-called Eurocentrism of past centuries and discovering the great and ancient religions of non-biblical peoples. But religious pluralism is not a new proposal. The attitude was rampant in the world into which Christianity was born. If the early Christians had been willing to include Christ in the pantheon of deities worshiped by the pagans, the martyrs would never have gone to their deaths, but the pagan world would never have been converted. The Roman senator Symmachus argued that religious truth had to be approached through a variety of faiths, but his views were vigorously repudiated by theologians such as Ambrose. As Paul had already declared in his diatribe against idolatry, the pagans have many gods and many lords, but Christians acknowledge only one God, the Father of all, and one Lord, Jesus Christ (1 Cor 8:4–6). Christianity stands or falls with the affirmation that, as there is but one God, so too there is but one name under heaven by whom one can be saved (Acts 4:12); for there is only one Mediator of salvation, the man Christ Jesus (1 Tim 2:5). To proclaim the gospel is necessarily to proclaim that Jesus Christ alone is Lord.

A sixth obstacle to evangelization is the false concept of freedom that pervades contemporary culture and frequently infects theologians. In the individualistic climate of our day, freedom is understood as the ability to choose whatever one pleases. Freedom of religion consequently means the capacity to choose whatever religion or lack of religion one wishes. This view has gained momentum as a reaction to situations in which the religion of the individual was made to depend almost totally upon the society into which one was born. In some countries, the control of religion was handed over to the rulers of the state, according to the axiom that the religion of the ruler is that of the people: *cuius regio eius religio.*

With the Enlightenment, the state ceased to favor any particular religion. For the past three hundred years, the political and social supports for religion have been crumbling. Ideological liberals seek to carry this secularization into the whole of public life, making faith a purely private matter to be settled in the intimacy of one's own conscience. On the theory that religion should always be a matter of personal choice, parents sometimes refrain from raising their children in a definite faith. For teachers or others to manifest their faith or to pray in public is today deplored as a form of proselytism. Evangelization is thus made socially unacceptable and in some circumstances illegal.

Theology should resist this privatization of religion. In the absence of favorable influences from parents, teachers, and the social environment, very few persons will find their way to a strong personal faith. Evangelization, to be sure, should not be done in an aggressive way that interferes with the religious freedom of the hearer but, when properly carried out, it can actually enhance that freedom. By presenting Christian faith as an inspiring, coherent, and credible option, it gives people the freedom to consider and adopt a faith that might otherwise elude them.

If faith were nothing more than a human opinion, and if it had no real consequences for salvation, there might be good reasons for telling people to follow their own inclination about whether they wanted to believe or not. But Christians are convinced that their faith is true, that it is revealed by God, and that God wants all men and women to come to knowledge of the truth (1 Tim 2:5). For this reason every believer has a duty to try to share the faith. We cannot compel people to believe, and should not try to do so, but there is every reason for helping people to come to a willing and responsible decision of faith. In the absence of truth, freedom is greatly diminished. As the Gospels tell us, the truth will make us free (John 8:32). Christ frees us from the slavery of sin and error and leads us into "the glorious freedom of the children of God" (Rom 8:21). A correct theological notion of freedom can overcome the privatist individualism that today inhibits the task of evangelization.

Closely connected with this false concept of freedom is a seventh and final aberration, an antiauthoritarianism that militates against evangelization, especially in its Catholic form. In the current climate, institutions are usually objects of suspicion. Regarding the Catholic Church as a vast and highly organized institution, many of our contemporaries feel reluctant to place their trust in it. In practice, however, those who reject religious authority usually adopt some other authority, often unconsciously and uncritically. In rejecting the authority of revealed religion, they are generally submitting to the authority of the secularist opposition, which has its own institutions and promotional organs. Because truth in religious matters is hard to come by, the choice of a faith is almost inevitably a choice among rival authorities.

The rejection of authority is more often a sign of adolescent rebellion than of maturity. As we mature, we learn to distinguish between reliable and unreliable authorities and to make a discriminating use of authority, but not to dispense with all authority. St. Thomas says very wisely that whereas arguments from merely human authority are weaker than rational demonstrations, arguments from the authority of divine revelation give the strongest possible grounds for assent (*ST* 1.1.8, ad 2).

Theologians themselves are sometimes overly suspicious of ecclesiastical authority. This seems to be a hazard of their profession. Whenever a new pronouncement comes from the Holy See, theologians feel called upon to judge whether it is right or wrong. I confess that I do not think it is my function to judge the authorities whom God has set over the Church. They have the commission and the charisms to safeguard the transmission of the faith. It is for them to judge theology, not to be judged by it. As a theologian, I am grateful that there is someone to correct me.

Evangelizers should not appeal, purely and simply, to the teaching authority of the Church. In an age suspicious of institutions, we shall do well to emphasize, as Paul and John did, the joy and freedom that come from a personal relationship to Christ. In comparison with Christ the ecclesiastical institutions are mere means. The spoken and written word of God can mediate faith, but faith goes out beyond the words to submit to the person of the revealer. An evangelically renewed Catholicism will seek to show that the entire apparatus of Catholicism, including the hierarchical ministry, the proclaimed word, and the sacraments, has value because and insofar as it gives more adequate and authentic access to the God who comes to us in Jesus Christ. Christ and his gospel must be proclaimed, in season and out of season. Evangelization is the primary and essential task of the Church. Those who have been successfully evangelized find their home in the Church as the place in which their relationship to Christ can be fully lived out. Through its ministries and sacraments, they have continually new access to the Holy Spirit, the Spirit of the living Christ.

In the last analysis, it is not individual Christians nor even the Church that proclaims Christ. According to a sounder theology of evangelization, Christ proclaims the gospel through the Church and its members. The Holy Spirit is the transcendent agent of evangelization. We strive to be obedient instruments. Since we cannot cause anyone to believe, we must accompany our efforts with prayer that God will bestow the grace of faith upon those to whom the gospel message is proclaimed.

Seeing itself as addressed by the call of recent popes for a new evangelization, contemporary theology can profit from the present moment as a season of grace. Directing its critical scrutiny upon itself, theology should be alert to root out any tendencies it may have had that stand in the way of evangelization. In becoming authentically evangelical, theology can better achieve its own objective, which is to understand and serve the faith that comes through Christ and the apostles. By opening itself more fully to the word of God, it can assist the Church to adhere to that word more faithfully and proclaim it more effectively, so that the whole world, in the words of Vatican II, "by hearing the message of salvation, may believe, and by believing may hope, and by hoping may love" (*DV* 1).

Chapter 8

Models of Evangelization

The Church always has to combat the danger of becoming too turned in upon herself, preoccupied with internal ecclesiastical problems and oblivious of her mission. At times, the Church appears more like the apostles before the Resurrection, cowering in the Upper Room with locked doors, than like the apostles boldly preaching the risen Christ on Pentecost. Thanks to the Great Commission given to her by the Lord before his Ascension, the Church is charged with the task of proclaiming the good news everywhere and to all.

We cannot simply wait for people to find their way into the Church on their own initiative. The message to be believed is a story to be told. Unless people hear it, they cannot be expected to believe it. Who except us, who are within the community of faith, can tell the world about Jesus Christ the Redeemer?

In our own day, the Catholic Church is growing, but hardly keeping pace with the growth of world population. In this country, the Catholic population would probably be shrinking except for immigration from Catholic countries. Meanwhile Evangelical Protestant and Pentecostal churches are rapidly expanding. They have retained the missionary spirit that belongs to Christianity by right.

Vatican II, or rather the popular interpretation of Vatican II, has something to do with the decline of Catholic evangelization. In spite of its strong statements on the primacy of Christ and the urgency of missionary activity, the Council seems to have drawn attention more to internal Catholic questions, such as collegiality, synodal structures, and regionalism. In speaking of persons and groups other than Catholics, the Council seemed to emphasize dialogue more than proclamation. In its efforts to be friendly to all, the Council encouraged a very optimistic view of other churches and religions, and even of secular movements, unintentionally giving the impression that there were many parallel ways of salvation available for those who were not Catholic.

In countries such as the United States, where individualism is dominant, the Council was heard as though it had been content to treat religion as a private matter to be settled by each individual in the intimacy of his or her own conscience. But in fact the Council was not content to remove religion from the public order and allow secular governments to ignore religious truth and revealed morality.

In previous chapters, we have seen how Popes Paul VI and John Paul II corrected many of the misunderstandings. Paul VI declared that all the objectives of the Council are "summed up in this single one: to make the Church of the twentieth century ever better fitted for proclaiming the Gospel to the people of the twentieth century" (*EN* 2). Evangelization, he asserted, is "the grace and vocation proper to the Church, her deepest identity" (*EN* 14). John Paul II agreed with Paul VI's interpretation of Vatican II. He called again for a renewal of missionary evangelization, describing it as "the primary service which the Church can render to every individual and to all humanity in the modern world" (*RMis* 2).

The recent popes, like Vatican II before them, have tirelessly proclaimed that Jesus Christ is the way, the truth, and the life. Without him, individual persons and societies cannot find the true way that leads to life. Those of us who been privileged to hear and believe the Christian message have a solemn responsibility to bear witness to it, for the glory of God and for the salvation of the world.

Many Christians, I believe, grant the importance of evangelization in theory but shy away from it in practice. Very often, I suspect, they have a narrow and inadequate conception of the meaning of the term. Perhaps they are put off by certain styles of evangelism. Sectarian Protestantism, they often feel, uses methods that are too aggressive; often it settles for merely verbal or emotional responses in which people profess an experience of Christ as their personal Savior.

In sharp contrast to this narrow concept, Catholicism looks upon evangelization as a complex process consisting of many elements. Among these elements, wrote Paul VI, are "the renewal of humanity, witness, explicit proclamation, inner adherence, entry into the community, acceptance of signs, apostolic initiative" (*EN* 24). For this reason, it may be useful to reflect on the different dimensions or styles of evangelization—the "models," if you like. In my own reflections, I have profited immensely from a doctoral dissertation recently completed at Fordham University, where I teach. The dissertation, written by Father Timothy E. Byerley, was published by the Paulist Press in 2008 under the title *The Great Commission*. While using my own titles, definitions, and examples, I would like to borrow from Father Byerley his six models of evangelization. In my own terminology the six means of evangelization will be: personal witness, proclamation by word, worship, community, inculturation, and works of charity.

Personal Witness

The first model, then, is personal witness, by which I mean the good example of a life totally dedicated to Christ. According to Paul VI, "The first means of evangelization is the witness of an authentically Christian life, given over to God in a communion that nothing should destroy and at the same time given to one's neighbor with limitless zeal" (*EN* 41). He also declares: "Such a witness is already a silent proclamation of the Good News and a very powerful and effective one. Here we have an initial act of evangelization" (*EN* 21).

Referring back to Paul VI, John Paul II asserts that "People today put more trust in witnesses than in teachers, in experience than in teaching, and in life and action than in theories. The witness of a Christian life is the first and irreplaceable form of mission" (*RMis* 42).

The preeminent form of personal witness is martyrdom. Beginning with Stephen, whose stoning seems to have made a deep impression on Paul, the martyrs have provoked admiration and won many to the faith. But witness more often takes place in less dramatic ways. One thinks in this connection of St. Francis of Assisi, who is said to have told his companions: "Preach the gospel every day, and if necessary use words." When he invited a friar to accompany him to preach in a neighboring village, the two of them walked to the village, passed through its streets, and returned without having addressed the people. The friar asked St. Francis, "When are we going to preach?" And St. Francis replied, "We have already done so by our appearance and demeanor." "That was a more powerful sermon," he added, "than if we had gone into the marketplace and harangued the people."[1]

I recall some years ago reading a brief memorandum by Walker Percy on his conversion. He mentioned particularly the example of a college classmate who used to steal off quietly each morning before breakfast to attend Mass. The manifest devotion of this classmate was a kind of silent sermon, more effective perhaps than any spoken admonition.

Proclamation by Word

The second model consists of verbal testimony in its various forms: initial proclamation, catechesis, apologetics, and the like. After discussing personal witness as the first form of evangelization, Paul VI adds that "even the finest witness will prove ineffective in the long run if it is not explained, justified...and made explicit by a clear and unequivocal proclamation of the Lord Jesus....There is no true evangelization if the name, the teaching, the life, the promises, the Kingdom and the mystery of Jesus of Nazareth, the Son of God, are not explained" (*EN* 22).

John Paul II, taking up this idea from Paul VI, states: "Proclamation is the permanent priority of mission. The Church cannot elude Christ's explicit mandate, nor deprive men and women of the 'Good News' about their being loved and saved by God" (*RMis* 44).

Beginning with Paul, Christianity has a long series of heralds who have courageously and tirelessly preached the gospel in difficult and dangerous circumstances. In this connection, we remember Saint Dominic, founder of the Order of Preachers, who labored among the heretics of southern France, and Francis Xavier, who traveled halfway round the globe in order to proclaim Christ in India, the East Indies, and Japan. Closer to our own time, we remember Pope John Paul II, who made himself a pilgrim pope in order to evangelize every continent.

Under the rubric of evangelization by word, we should include the great writers who evangelized not so much by the spoken word as by the power of the pen. Countless converts owe their Christian faith to authors such as John Henry Newman, G. K. Chesterton, and C. S. Lewis.

In opposition to the idea that dialogue has become preferable to proclamation, the popes have asserted that there can be no conflict between proclaiming Christ and engaging in interreligious dialogue. While acknowledging all that is true and good in Buddhism, Hinduism, and Islam, for example, the Church insists that Christ alone is the way, the truth, and the life, and that membership in the Church remains the ordinary means of salvation (*RMis* 55; cf. *EN* 53). Dialogue does not require that these contentious points be withheld.

Worship

The third model of evangelization is Christian worship. Worship is of course an activity of the believing community directed primarily to God; it is not conducted for the sake of making an impression on outsiders. But perhaps for that very reason it does make an impression on outsiders who become aware of it. They are struck by the intensity and sincerity of the Church's relationship to God.

As a first example, I may mention the letter of John Adams to his wife Abigail in which he speaks of the Catholic service he attended in Philadelphia at the time of the Constitutional Convention. After describing the service, he commented: "Here is every Thing which can lay hold of the Eye, Ear, and Imagination. Every Thing which can charm and bewitch the simple and ignorant. I wonder how Luther ever broke the spell." Although he personally resisted the attraction, Adams felt the power of the liturgy to communicate a sense of mystery and raise the spirits of the congregation to God.[2]

St. Elizabeth Ann Seton, when she was in Leghorn with her dying husband, observed with wonder and with a kind of envy the devotion of the Catholic population to the Blessed Sacrament. When it was carried in procession beneath her window, she found herself kneeling in adoration. Her admiration for Catholic worship led her to study Catholic doctrine and eventually to become a dedicated Catholic and a sainted religious.

If a third example be needed, I can mention John Henry Newman. In the course of his voyage to Italy and especially to Sicily in 1833, he was deeply impressed by the crowds attending Mass in the early hours of the morning, raising their voices in hymns to God. Without yet being able to accept the truth of Catholic doctrine, he came to the realization that the Church of Rome was capable of arousing "feelings of awe, mystery, tenderness, reverence, devotedness, and other feelings which may especially be called Catholic."[3] The pious worshipers who so impressed Newman had no realization that they were engaged in evangelization; they would have been greatly surprised to learn that they were playing a part in the conversion of the most celebrated theologian of the century.

In the course of the next few years, Newman came to feel that he and his colleagues in the Oxford Movement were erecting a "paper church"—one that existed in the writings of theologians but had no living congregations behind it. The Church, he knew, must be a worshiping community.

Worship is connected with evangelization not only because of its influence on outsiders, but also because of what it does for the community itself. The liturgy of the sacraments, which includes the homily, immerses the participants in the mystery of Christ and thereby helps them to center their lives on Christ and to become heralds and bearers of the gospel message when they return to their ordinary occupations.

Community

As a fourth model of evangelization, Father Byerley proposes community. Confronted by the anonymity of our secularized and mechanized world, many people find themselves searching for interpersonal community. In the Greco-Roman world in which Christianity originally developed, much the same was true. The Protestant sociologist Rodney Stark, in his historical study *The Rise of Christianity*, points out the cruelty and inhumanity of ancient paganism. Women, children, and elderly persons were treated without respect and without mercy. Christianity, Stark maintains, grew because "Christians constituted an intense community, able to generate the 'invincible obstinacy' that so offended the young Pliny but yielded immense rewards. And the primary means of its growth was through the united and motivated efforts of the growing numbers of Christian believers, who invited their friends, relatives, and neighbors to share 'the good news.'"[4]

In the twentieth century a similar dynamic came to the surface. A variety of new movements originated in the Catholic Church. In Europe and the United States we saw the birth of the Focolare, the Neo-Catechumenal Way, the Charismatic Renewal, and others. Something of the same motivation, I suspect, accounts for the success of enterprises such as San Egidio in Rome and the basic ecclesial communities of Latin America. Communities such as these evangelize not so much by going out and recruiting new members as by exercising a force of attraction that makes people want to come in. If the Church is seen as a cordial community of love and mutual support, in which all have but one heart and one soul, it will attract new members almost without trying.

Inculturation

As his fifth model of evangelization, Father Byerley proposes inculturation, meaning the incarnation of the gospel in the cultural forms familiar and intelligible to those being evangelized. A paradigmatic instance of inculturation is the transposition of Christianity from Jewish to Greco-Roman soil, which began already when Paul had a vision bidding him to come to Macedonia. When Paul visited Athens, he was invited to speak at the Areopagus, the cultural center of the intelligentsia. His sermon, as summarized in the seventeenth chapter of Acts, is a model of inculturated evangelization. After referring to the altars to the Greek gods and quoting Greek poetry, he went on to challenge them with the good news of Christ's bodily resurrection.

In the early Middle Ages, Benedictine monks such as Augustine of Canterbury showed great sensitivity to the cultures and traditions of England and Gaul. As Pope John Paul II explains in his encyclical *Slavorum apostoli*, Saints Cyril and Methodius did much the same for the parts of eastern Europe they evangelized. In early modern times, Jesuits such as Matteo Ricci and Roberto di Nobili were extraordinarily successful in clothing Christianity with the cultural forms of China and India. In the United States, authors such as Orestes Brownson and Isaac Hecker in the nineteenth century and John Courtney Murray in the twentieth did much to make the Catholic faith at home on the American scene.

Paul VI in his apostolic exhortation on evangelization called attention to the problems of relating the Christian message to contemporary culture. Conscious that modern culture is in many ways resistant to the gospel, Paul VI avoided terms such as "inculturation," which could be taken to suggest that the culture is a satisfactory vessel for Christian faith. On the ground that cultures need to be regenerated by an encounter with the gospel, he spoke by preference of the evangelization of cultures as an imperative for our time (*EN* 20). John Paul II in his missionary encyclical *Redemptoris missio* uses the term *inculturation* but defines it in such a way as to include the transformation of the values already present in the culture and their integration into Christianity (*RMis* 52).

John Paul raises questions about the Areopagi of our day. Where, he asks, are the cultural sectors in which the gospel still needs to be proclaimed (*RMis* 37)? The first such Areopagus, he says, is the world of communications, including the mass media, which exerts an enormous influence on everyone, perhaps especially the young. Among other new cultural sectors he mentions scientific research, human rights, and international relations. These fields of study and action have immense potentialities for good or evil. To prevent our civilization from sinking ever deeper into consumerism and materialism, the pope warns, these Areopagi need to be transformed by contact with the gospel. They cannot be evangelized simply from outside, by words of admonition; the evangelization must come from within, by committed Christians thoroughly familiar with the relevant disciplines.

Works of Charity

The sixth and last of the models of evangelization I am proposing may be called works of charity, or perhaps the social apostolate. In the New Testament itself we read of Paul's efforts to bring material aid to the Christians of Jerusalem by means of a collection from the missionary communities. Pope Benedict XVI in his encyclical *Deus caritas est* reminds his readers that Julian the Apostate, the fourth-century emperor who abandoned Christianity in favor of a revived paganism, singled out the Church's charitable activity as the prime reason for the popularity of the "Galileans." In a spirit of competition, he strove to make similar good works a feature of his restored paganism (*DCE* 24).

Down through the centuries, the Church has been a leader in caring for orphans and widows, for the sick and the aged. She has been conspicuous for establishing schools, hospitals, and relief programs. In recent memory, Dorothy Day, through her Catholic Worker movement, drew many to the Church. Even more recently, Blessed Teresa of Calcutta captured the attention of the world by her apostolate to the sick and the dying. She did not seek to make her patients Catholics, but the example of her selfless charity drew many to the Church. Malcolm Muggeridge, for instance, describes her as a major influence on his conversion. But above all, he wrote, "It was the Catholic Church's firm stand against contraception and abortion which finally made me decide to become a Catholic." The following paragraph is so eloquent that I cannot resist quoting it:

> Contraception and abortion have made havoc for both the young and the old. The terrible things that are going on, the precocious sexual practices of children, the debaucheries in universities, making eroticism an end and not a means, are a consequence of violating the natural order of things. As the Romans treated eating as

an end in itself, making themselves sick in a vomitorium, so as to enable them to return to the table and stuff themselves with more delicacies, so people now end up in a sort of sexual vomitorium. The Church's stand is absolutely correct. It is to its eternal honour that it opposed contraception, even if the opposition failed. I think, historically, people will say it was a very gallant effort to prevent a moral disaster.[5]

The Catholic Church's opposition to abortion was crucial also in the conversion of Bernard Nathanson, who had been the director of the largest abortion clinic in the United States and had overseen some 75,000 abortions in his pro-choice career. The development of ultrasound led him to reconsider his opinions and join the pro-life movement. Attending a number of protests sponsored by Operation Rescue, an ecumenical organization, he noted what he later described as the "indefinable air of selflessness, even genuine altruism" with which the protesters sang hymns and prayed. Their faith enabled them to sit "serene and unafraid at the epicenter of legal, physical, ethical, and moral chaos."[6] The experience led him to think seriously about God and before long to join the Catholic Church.

The stance of the Church on public issues such as abortion raises the question of Catholic social teaching. In his encyclical *Sollicitudo rei socialis* and elsewhere John Paul II declared that social teaching is a means of evangelization (*SRS* 41). Evangelization in its full amplitude includes the doctrine of human rights, the promotion of the common good, and everything that can help to build a civilization of love. Although evangelization may never be reduced to the dimensions of a mere temporal project, the gospel has necessary implications regarding peace and justice in the human community. It goes far beyond the limits of the sanctuary and the cloister. Lay persons have a special responsibility to evangelize secular society, including the workplace and the public square. The values of the gospel can vivify and transform human relations in law, politics, business, and all the professions.

Once evangelization is seen in its full dimensions, it becomes evident that it is not the concern of one special group of Christians.

Some may have an aptitude and inclination to engage in explicit proclamation, which is always necessary. But others may evangelize in unobtrusive ways, by living out their Christian vocation to the full. You may be called to give silent witness, prompting others to wonder why your fidelity to the rule of prayer is so important to you. You may be gifted in building up small communities of Bible study or works of charity toward persons in need. You may be gifted as a writer or a scientist, as a politician or a statesman, as a master of electronic communications, or as a financier. Every one of these callings, pursued with a Christian inspiration, has its place within the panoply of missionary endeavors.

Notwithstanding the varieties, evangelization has one and the same center and driving force. It flows from the love of Christ, who continues to act every day through the Holy Spirit. By returning constantly to him as its source and goal, evangelization can always remain fresh and vibrant. Pope John Paul said once that faith is strengthened when it is given to others. Conversely, we may add, faith is weakened when we hoard it to ourselves.

Notes

1. I have found a couple of versions of this legend on the Internet, thanks to Yahoo.

2. John Adams, Letter to Abigail of October 9, 1774, in *The Book of Abigail and John: Selected Letters of the Adams Family 1762–1784* (Cambridge, MA: Harvard University Press, 1975), 78–79.

3. John Henry Newman, *Apologia Pro Vita Sua*, ed. Ian Ker (London: Penguin, 1994), 157. Newman is quoting from a letter written by him at the time.

4. Rodney Stark, *The Rise of Christianity* (Princeton, NJ: Princeton University Press, 1996), 208.

5. Malcolm Muggeridge, *Confessions of a Twentieth-Century Pilgrim* (San Francisco: Harper & Row, 1988), 140–41.

6. Bernard Nathanson, *The Hand of God* (Washington, DC: Regnery, 1996), 191–93.

Chapter 9

Models of Catechesis

Catechesis is not wholly distinct from evangelization; indeed, it may be called the second stage, following upon primary evangelization, in which the basic elements of the faith are proclaimed. The catechetical process appears to me to be extremely important for the future of the Church in this country and all over the world. We face enormous difficulties in transmitting the Catholic faith to new generations in the present atmosphere of secularism, relativism, and postmodernism.

In the course of my adult life, I have observed a succession of radical changes in the methods of religious instruction. In the days before Vatican II the primary instrument was a printed text such as the *Baltimore Catechism*, which encapsulated the dogmatic teaching of the Church in question-and-answer format. But complaints were already being heard at that time that the approach failed to elicit real personal assent from the students. In western Europe some theologians devised a new proclamatory (or "kerygmatic") style of theology that could be used as an alternative for the reigning Scholastic approach. This new theology took as its paradigm the sermons of Peter and Paul in the early chapters of Acts, which confidently proclaimed the great deeds of God in salvation history and called for a response of praise and worship.

In the late 1950s, Catholics were inclined to structure religious education around salvation history, emphasizing prophetically interpreted events rather than eternal truths and doctrinal propositions, as the older catechisms had done. In many cases, this style was combined with a liturgical approach that emphasized the actualization of the mysteries of faith in the Church's worship. The historical-liturgical approach had hardly gotten underway when it was overtaken in the mid-sixties by a new experiential approach, which encouraged students to reflect on their own experiences as places they could best find God. Since the mid-1970s, the experiential model has been yielding to a so-called praxis model, which uses the gospel to engage in social criticism.

The efforts to produce new and revolutionary catechisms in some cases led to excesses. Cardinal Ratzinger, reflecting on the situation in 1985, complained: "The new texts, with their hasty *aggiornamento*, had themselves already begun to look dated; it is inevitable that whoever binds himself too rashly to today already looks old-fashioned tomorrow....As a matter of fact, the real result of this process of ever-new adaptations was an emptying-out of catechesis." Some of the current catechesis, he said, had almost no content but simply revolved around itself. The power and beauty of the Christian message were almost lost from view.[1]

The Synod of Bishops in 1985, noting the confusion in current catechesis, reported: "Very many have expressed the desire that a catechism or compendium of all Catholic doctrine regarding both faith and morals be composed, that it might be, as it were, a point of reference for the catechisms that are prepared for the various regions. The presentation of doctrine must be biblical and liturgical. It must be sound doctrine suited to the present life of Christians"[2] The result was the *Catechism of the Catholic Church*, which was completed in its first edition in 1992. The Church is now producing a new crop of catechisms and textbooks for various nations, age groups, and language groups that are being scrutinized by the bishops for their conformity with the *Catechism of the Catholic Church*.

The United States Conference of Catholic Bishops has set up an Ad Hoc Committee to Oversee the Use of the Catechism. Under the direction of this committee a *United States Catholic Catechism for Adults* has already been produced. The committee has also been conducting a review of catechetical materials in use in our country on the high school level. In the judgment of this committee, many of the current texts are seriously deficient from a doctrinal point of view.[3]

While intended as a point of reference, the universal catechism does not purport to establish the structure and style of catechetical programs and religion textbooks. Educators are free to organize the materials in different ways for different groups of students. To indicate the various ways in which this has been done, it may be useful to present some models that seem to show up in the literature familiar to me. My five models will be ideal types. Most religious educators, I am aware, combine two or more of the models.

Doctrinal

The first model is the doctrinal, which is exemplified by practically all of the approved Catholic catechisms published between the Council of Trent and the Second Vatican Council, though we should not imagine that catechists confined themselves to this one approach. The most familiar example for most of us might be the *Baltimore Catechism*, which was in use in the United States for seventy years before Vatican II. It focuses on the teaching of popes and councils concerning faith and morals and is designed to arm the student against Protestant errors.

The doctrinal model relies heavily on the authority of Scripture and the Magisterium of the Church, but it usually includes an apologetical ingredient, which seeks to show that the teachings of the Church are worthy of belief. In its moral teaching, this approach makes use of natural reason as well as Christian revelation. Much of the Church's moral teaching is accessible through the natural law as knowable by reason.

The objective of religious education in this approach is to produce Christians who are confident and orthodox in their Catholic faith and well equipped to answer Protestant objections. It is hoped that their understanding of pure doctrine will motivate them to conduct themselves virtuously.

This first approach produced generations of Catholics who were familiar with the basic contents of the faith. The question-and-answer format gave them a well-stocked memory of important truths that they could later come to appreciate. Yet the system had its critics. They complained that everything was taught on the same level as though common opinions of theologians stood on the same level as defined dogmas. Memory, they said, was emphasized more than understanding. For many students the content was too abstract; their emotions and imagination were left untouched. The method presupposed that the students had previously been evangelized, but often this was not the case. The system therefore produced not a few unevangelized but well-catechized Catholics.

The new *Catechism of the Catholic Church* sought to remedy many of these defects. In the spirit of Vatican II, it strove to recover the hierarchy of revealed truths, not all of which are equally fundamental. It accorded primacy to the mysteries of the Trinity and the Incarnation. It made extensive use of Holy Scripture and dropped the polemical stance of post-Tridentine catechisms. Not content to supply the bare bones of doctrine, it included inspiring quotations from the Fathers, the liturgy, and the writings of the saints. After treating fundamental beliefs according to the sequence of the creed, the *CCC* in later sections gave corresponding attention to sacramental worship, the Christian life, and prayer, treating these last three topics for their own sake, rather than reducing them to doctrine.[4] The *CCC* therefore gives a compendium of Christian doctrine that retains the merits of previous doctrinal catechisms but opens the way for other approaches.

Kerygamtic

The second model came into Catholic theology between the two world wars. I have already mentioned the kerygmatic movement. It originated in Austria with Josef A. Jungmann and was widely publicized by Johannes Hofinger among others. Valerian Cardinal Gracias summarized the decisive influence of Jungmann's book *The Good News and Our Proclamation of the Faith* as follows:

> Since the publication of this book in 1936, catechesis has been directed toward this central theme. Our religion is an organic unit, in which we must discern a fundamental core which we have to proclaim emphatically (*kerysso*—to proclaim). This core is the message of Christ, "the mystery which hath been hidden from ages and generations but now is manifested to his saints" (Col 1:26). Our way back to the Father is in union with

Christ, through the working of the Holy Spirit. All the other truths of our religion have to be explained from this standpoint and with this perspective. What we have to preach is the gospel—the good news that Christ is among us.[5]

This second approach received a measure of support from Vatican II's *Dogmatic Constitution on Divine Revelation,* which opened with a summons to proclaim the word of God confidently (*DV* 1). In its first chapter, it traced the main lines of biblical salvation history, which culminated in the death and resurrection of Christ and the sending of the Spirit of truth (*DV* 4). It defined faith as an act by which we entrust our whole selves to God (*DV* 5).

In this second model the approach was concrete rather than abstract, narrative rather than doctrinal. Its proclamatory style was well suited to elicit acts of personal faith. By its clear focus on the Paschal mystery, kerygmatic catechesis spared the student from becoming burdened by a seemingly endless catalogue of truths to be believed. All this was accomplished without falling into subjectivism. Like the first model, the second recognized that faith was a response to God's free self-revelation. Though primarily focused on biblical events, the kerygmatic model could easily be extended to include a consideration of the Church as it developed over the centuries from the Christ-event through a dramatic series of historical challenges.

Notwithstanding these and other merits, the kerygmatic model in pure form did not satisfy every need. Peter and Paul, in their early sermons in Acts, were preaching to Jews who already accepted the reality of God and were alert to detect signs of his action in salvation history. Applied today, the model seemed to require a considerable process of preevangelization that would dispose students to respond to the Christian kerygma.[6] Many of them needed to be rescued from a secularist worldview that left no place for a God who speaks and acts. Besides, the whole corpus of Catholic doctrine could not easily be fitted into the framework of the kerygma. The creed seemed to offer a more adequate outline.

The evangelistic style of the kerygmatic model took proper cognizance of the fact that faith is normally transmitted by the testimony of committed believers. But religious instruction is often conducted in the classroom or other settings in which proclamation seems inappropriate. Many teachers are understandably reluctant to assume the role of preachers. Knowledge can be tested in examinations; personal faith cannot.

Compared with the doctrinal model, the kerygmatic had the advantage of a narrative style, which many students find more interesting. The story of the great deeds of God in history, moreover, is richer and more vivid than the doctrines that can be distilled out of it. Many students, however, felt that by locating revelation so far in the past, salvation history was alienating. They yearned to encounter the God who transforms and saves us today.

Liturgical

The second model therefore called for completion by a third, which I call the liturgical or mystagogical. The celebration of the sacraments brings the past events of salvation history, including the Paschal mystery, into the here-and-now. The presence of God in the celebration calls for a personal response that is authentically religious. By encountering the Holy in the liturgy, the student has the experience of entering the realm of the divine. The third model was not difficult to combine with the second because the founders of kerygmatic catechesis (men like Jungmann and Hofinger) were also liturgical theologians.

Worship is often depicted as the primary cradle of doctrine. The fifth-century theologian Prosper of Aquitaine formulated the principle, "The law of prayer establishes the law of believing." Pius XII, however, pointed out in his encyclical *Mediator Dei* that the priorities are mutual. While right worship is the school of right belief, right belief gives rise to correct worship.

As Edward Yarnold explains in his helpful book, *The Awe-Inspiring Rites of Initiation*, bishops who preached catechetical and mystagogical sermons in patristic times, such as Cyril of Jerusalem and Ambrose of Milan, made extensive use of the symbolism of the rites of initiation, including the ceremonies of baptism, confirmation, and the Eucharist.[7] The catechumenate, which was timed to reached its climax in Holy Week, contained numerous blessings, exorcisms, anointings, vigils, and penitential rites that were rich in symbolism. Baptism was conducted in the dead of night, with total immersion in the font, followed by the donning of new white garments and the presentation of a lighted candle to each candidate. These and other ceremonies provided occasions for instruction packed with biblical references and doctrinal reflections. Because the candidates were required to recite the creed and the Lord's Prayer, and to know the Ten Commandments, these texts likewise became central to prebaptismal catechesis. The three-fold immersion of the baptized in the name of the Father, the Son, and the Holy Spirit called attention to the salvific importance of the mystery of the Trinity.

The restoration of the catechumenate in 1972 led to a revival of the mystagogical style of instruction. The Rite of Christian Initiation of Adults uses communal worship as the recommended setting for the instruction of adult converts. For younger students who are being brought up in the Catholic faith, the liturgy likewise provides a very suitable context for catechesis. Liturgical vestments, church architecture, the structure of the Mass, the various rites of the Church, and the seasons and feasts of the liturgical year can serve as reference points.

This liturgical context has the advantage of inducing a religious frame of mind in the students, evoking an attitude of reverent hearing. Unlike abstract doctrine, it speaks to them directly, evoking their present relationship to God. Unlike the kerygmatic model, the sacramental goes beyond the contingent facts of history to facilitate an encounter with God himself, the source and end of all creation. The sacraments, as signs imbued with the power of what they signify, have a pedagogical force that surpasses mere words.

The liturgical model of catechesis, for all its merits, fails to provide a total answer to the problems of religious education. With its emphasis on sacred history, sacred places, and sacred ceremonies, it could easily lead to a neglect of the secular. The Second Vatican Council, in its *Pastoral Constitution on the Church in the Modern World*, mentioned the separation between faith and daily life as one of the more serious errors of our age (*GS* 43). During the 1960s, many young students felt themselves irresistibly drawn to the secular world with all its enticements and its possibilities for good. The extraordinary popularity of Harvey Cox's *The Secular City* is a convenient symbol of the triumph of the secular over the sacred that many people took to be a sign of the times.

Experiential

Catholic religious educators accommodated themselves in various degrees to this new situation. Seeking to build on what was positive in it, they developed a fourth model of religious instruction. Marcel van Caster, in his 1964 work *The Structure of Catechetics*, noted that because God speaks through the signs of the times, catechesis ought to search into the Christian significance of secular events. But he cautioned that secular events are not to be taken as direct revelations of God; they need to be interpreted in light of the revelation already given in Christ.[8] In a book published in 1968, translated under the title *Experiential Catechetics*, he wrote more extensively on this theme. Revelation, he explained, could be mediated in two ways—the sacred and the profane.

Men and women of our day, he believed, are more responsive to the second because they think in terms of experience. Catechetics must therefore help them to develop their understanding of experience in the light of Christian revelation. Instruction that sets forth God's word as found in the biblical message and the liturgy, he maintained, needs to be complemented by instruction that interprets the present situation and relates it to Christ.[9] Van Caster insisted, however, that the religious meaning of present events could not be reliably discerned except in light of Christ and the gospel. Experiential catechetics required students already familiar with the good news of God's revelation in Christ as taught in more traditional forms of catechesis—notably the kerygmatic and the liturgical.

There were many varieties of experiential catechesis. Pierre Babin took the genre in a psychological direction, taking account of the age of students and recommending a pedagogy of discovery in place of transmission. For such a pedagogy, he wrote, "it is absolutely necessary that our students experience the faith as a kingdom, a promised land, as salvation for themselves today."[10] In the United States, Gabriel Moran contended that experience itself is revelational.[11] Instead of searching for the revealed word in ancient sources, Moran maintained, students should be taught to discover the meaning of their own lives as religious. In place of Christian catechesis—a term that smacked too much of indoctrination—Moran preferred to speak of religious education, a process that would dispose students to make free and intelligent decisions in a world that offered a great variety of religious options.[12]

James Michael Lee asserts, like Moran, that theology has little to contribute to religious education. Opposing the tendency to make catechesis a "head trip," he advocates greater attention to the affections and to the body. "The task of the religion class," he writes, "is so to structure and recast the learner's experience that God's ongoing revelation is consciously, meaningfully, and affectively incorporated into the person's self-system and behavioral patterns of action."[13] According to Lee, the classroom should be made into "a laboratory and a workshop for Christian living where students learn Christian living by engaging in Christian living in the here-and-now learning situation."[14]

During the 1970s, this experiential trend was carried to great lengths in many classrooms. Finding little response to other approaches, religion teachers focused on contemporary experience, allowing their students to remain ignorant of the basic facts of sacred history and the primary articles of the creed. To judge from what I have been told by experts in the field, textbooks fell out of use; the students themselves became the primary text. Their teachers asked them to express their feelings about life, and the students felt bored.

New winds from Latin America seem to have roused religious education out of its introspective phase. Liberation theology shared with experiential catechesis a preoccupation with the topical and the secular, but it added an element of social consciousness that could claim to have strong roots in Catholic tradition. Many theologians in Central and South America were concerned by the abject poverty of the masses. They felt that religious education in the past had been too exclusively theoretical, meaning by this that it had unduly separated knowledge from action. Borrowing some insights from Hegel and Marx, they contended that we know best by doing and that orthopraxis was the proper route to orthodoxy.

Praxis

The Brazilian Paolo Freire gave powerful expression to the educational implications of this new theology in his influential work, *The Pedagogy of the Oppressed*.[15] He protests against what he calls the "banking model" of education, in which the teacher deposits knowledge into the minds of the students, who receive it passively. Freire recommended a problem-posing model of education in which teachers and students together reflect on their actual life situations with a critical eye. The aim was to raise the students' consciousness to the point where they would be able to engage in corrective action leading to social change.

Although Freire did not work explicitly in the field of religious education, religious educators were not slow to profit from his ideas. Many of them considered that catechesis had been too individualistic, too indifferent to social injustices, and too neglectful of the future. Christians, they felt, should be formed in ways that would incite them to build a new world, to taking part in the growth of the kingdom of God here on earth. Praxis in this model predominated over mere theory.

In the United States the most prominent representative of this new form of religious pedagogy is Thomas Groome, who promotes "shared Christian praxis." He describes his method as "a group of Christians sharing in dialogue their critical reflection in light of the Christian Story and its Vision toward the end of lived Christian faith."[16] In this definition, the object of critical reflection is not so much a sacred text as the reality of present action. In order that the resulting knowledge may be our own and not simply a report of what others say, the action must be one in which we ourselves participate. But the action is not a solitary one; it is a communal enterprise performed by a group of Christians. They are to be in dialogue, respectfully listening to one another and ready to learn from their partners. The dialogue is to be a critical one, in which the participants try to discern what ought to be retained and what ought to be changed in the existing situation. The criterion is twofold: the Christian Story and the Christian Vision. The Story is the biblical narrative and the history of the Church, consisting of all the lives and events that have occurred as believers have attempted to live in obedience to the precepts and example of Jesus Christ. The Story, Groome insists, is not a mere fable; it consists of actual historical events. The Vision is the promised kingdom of God that is the calling and the hope of all Christians.

In comparison with the other models we have examined, Groome's position is inclusive. He does not set praxis in opposition to *theoria*, since he recognizes that praxis must take the Christian Story and the Christian Vision as its standards. He accepts the necessity of doctrine. Magisterial teaching, he states, is needed to keep the Church faithful to her apostolic origins as she develops in the course of centuries. In the absence of a magisterium, Groome remarks, "theology is a maze of conflicting opinions and different schools of thought and by itself a confusing ground for decisions of faith."[17] He remarks, however, that the magisterium must inform itself of the findings of the scholarly community and must seek to express consensus positions.

In agreement with the kerygmatic school, Groome acknowledges the centrality of the biblical story culminating in the death and resurrection of Christ and the sending of the Holy Spirit. He objects, however, that the Catholic kerygmatic theologians, like their Protestant neo-orthodox counterparts, give little place to the students' lived experience.[18]

Groome's observations on the experiential model are of interest. He shares with the experiential school a desire to take account of the lived experience of the student. He insists, however, that present experience be subjected to critical reflection. It must be held in critical correlation with the Story and the Vision, which can be imparted most effectively, he believes, by his method of shared Christian praxis.[19]

In Groome's praxis model the liturgical or mystagogical element receives some, but relatively little, attention. He speaks of liturgy as a remembrance and embodiment of the Christian story. In the Eucharist, he writes, our recalling of God's saving intervention in Jesus Christ becomes for us a saving event today.[20] His approach could be strengthened by exploiting the pedagogical potentialities of the restored catechumenate and the Rite of Christian Initiation of Adults.

Concluding Thoughts

The five models of catechesis I have presented all have their merits, inasmuch as they represent valid dimensions of integral Christian formation. It will be the task of religious educators, who know the needs, capacities, and limitations of their students, to structure the curriculum and make the necessary adaptations.

The entire process, I believe, may profitably take guidance from the *Catechism of the Catholic Church*, which felicitously combines the various components. Since religious education characteristically takes place in academic settings, the doctrinal element will normally be prominent. Its importance is evident from the definition given in the *Catechism*: "Catechesis is an education in the faith of children, young people, and adults which includes especially the teaching of Christian doctrine imparted, generally speaking, in an organic and systematic way, with a view to initiating the hearers into the fullness of Christian life" (*CCC* 5).

Doctrine should be taught with an emphasis on the great deeds of God in salvation history and with what God continues to do in the sacraments today. The kerygmatic and mystagogical elements should therefore be integrated into the doctrinal. Christian praxis may be incorporated as opportunity arises, especially for adult students who are socially involved. At every age level, account should be taken of the students' moral and religious experience. Teachers should make them conscious of the desire for the divine that God has implanted in every human heart and should build on the further experiences that faith itself engenders. In this connection, the religious educator may draw inspiration from the final part of the *CCC*, which deals with the life of prayer.

While seeking to keep informed of the changing theories of religious education, Christian catechists will take care not to allow their preoccupation with the latest methods and techniques to overshadow the abiding content of Christian faith. Presented in its organic unity, the Christian message has unceasing power to excite the enthusiasm of students and transform their lives. Catechists are called to be privileged instruments through whom God continues his saving work today. The success of their efforts will depend not on themselves alone but more crucially on the grace of God and the freely given response of the students. When the seed falls on fertile ground, a rich harvest may come forth. The evangelist may sow the seed; the catechist may water the growing plant, but only God can give the increase.

Notes

1. Joseph Ratzinger, *Introduction to Catechism of the Catholic Church* (San Francisco: Ignatius, 1994), 12–14.

2. Synod of Bishops, Extraordinary Assembly of 1985, "Final Report," IIB4; *Origins* 15 (December 19, 1985): 444–50, at 448.

3. Archbishop Alfred Hughes, "The State of High School Catechetical Texts," *Origins* 33 (November 20, 2003): 417–20.

4. The Roman Catechism had already been structured according to the headings of the Twelve Articles of the Creed, the Seven Sacraments, the Ten Commandments, and the Seven Petitions of the Lord's Prayer, but the emphasis remained on doctrine throughout.

5. Valerian Cardinal Gracias, "Modern Catechetical Renewal and the Missions," in *Teaching All Nations*, ed. Johannes Hofinger (New York: Herder and Herder, 1961), 13.

6. The Study Week on Mission Catechesis held at Bangkok in 1962 recommended a process consisting of three phases: preevangelization, the kerygma, and catechesis proper. See Alfonso M. Nebreda, *Kerygma in Crisis?* (Chicago: Loyola University Press, 1965).

7. Edward Yarnold, *The Awe-Inspiring Rites of Initiation: The Origins of the R.C.I.A.*, 2nd ed. (Collegeville, MN: Liturgical Press, 1994).

8. Marcel van Caster, *The Structure of Catechetics* (New York: Herder and Herder, 1965), 84–89. The original edition of this work was published in Bruges in 1964.

9. Jean Le Du and Marcel van Caster, *Experiential Catechetics* (Paramus, NJ: Newman, 1969), 154. The original edition of this work was published in Bruges in 1968.

10. Pierre Babin, *Options: Approaches for the Religious Education of Adolescents* (New York: Herder and Herder, 1967), 29.

11. Gabriel Moran, *The Present Revelation* (New York, Herder and Herder, 1972), 222–29.

12. Gabriel Moran, *Religious Body* (New York: Seabury, 1974), 149–54. See the discussion of "Religious Education and Gabriel Moran" in Mary Boys, *Educating in Faith: Maps and Visions* (San Francisco: Harper & Row, 1989), 126–28.

13. James Michael Lee, *The Shape of Religious Instruction* (Dayton, OH: Pflaum, 1971), 16.

14. Ibid., 19.

15. Paolo Freire, *The Pedagogy of the Oppressed* (New York: Seabury, 1970); original Portuguese edition, 1968.

16. Thomas H. Groome, *Christian Religious Education* (San Francisco: Jossey-Bass, 1980), 184.

17. Ibid., 200.

18. Ibid., 148.

19. Ibid., 149.

20. Ibid., 192.

Chapter 10

Models of Apologetics

Apologetics is not strictly a part of evangelization, but is intimately connected with it. The evangelist must in some way show that the message is credible—that there are good grounds for believing it to be true. Apologetics as a special discipline seeks to spell out these reasons in a systematic way and thereby to assist and support evangelization.

Apologetics has a long and venerable history, which starts in the New Testament itself. The apostles, commissioned to proclaim the gospel to the whole world, felt obliged to tell others why they too should believe. They told the Jews that Jesus was the fulfillment of the prophetic promises in the Old Testament, and that he had manifestly risen from the dead. In preaching to pagans, Paul told them that the God of Israel was the "unknown God" whom they worshiped in ignorance, the God of whom their poets wrote that "in him we live and move and have our being" (Acts 17:22–28). The first letter of Peter admonishes Christians to be ready at all times to give a defense of the hope that is in them (1 Pet 3:15).

Apologetics—in the sense of a reasoned defense of Christian faith—was strenuously cultivated by the Church Fathers, beginning with the apologists of the second century, such as Justin and Tertullian. In the Western tradition, Augustine and Aquinas, while they did not use the term *apologetics,* wrote at great length to show why it is reasonable to assent to the Christian faith. In the Middle Ages, Christian apologetics was directed especially to, or more often against, two religious groups: Jews and Muslims. A great deal of effort was expended to show both groups that the Old Testament predicted a Messiah, and that Jesus fulfilled the messianic promises. The Muslims were told, in addition, that Mohammed did not fulfill the Old Testament prophecies as Jesus did.

The great age of apologetics began in the seventeenth century, when Deist philosophers objected that revelation and faith were unnecessary because all the essential truths about God, the soul, and the moral law could be demonstrated by reason alone. Theologians argued in reply that revelation is necessary for a knowledge of saving truth. But at the same time apologists had to answer skeptics and agnostics who asserted that reason is incompetent to establish the existence of God, religion, and morality. Thus the apologists battled simultaneously on two fronts. First, they had to contend against the skeptics that reason could demonstrate certain basic religious truths, such as the existence of God and the possibility and knowability of revelation, if God were to give it. Then they had to argue against the rationalists that reason needed the help of revelation in order to find the way to eternal life. Only after these preambles could they proceed to demonstrate that the necessary revelation was given in biblical religion, culminating in Jesus Christ. Some apologists took a further step and tried to prove that a particular variety of Christianity (Catholic or Protestant) was the right one.

Throughout the nineteenth and early twentieth centuries, Protestants and Catholics alike placed high value on apologetics, producing many hundreds of ponderous and erudite tomes that were read with great eagerness by a broad public. On the whole, these works followed the standard approach that had been worked out since the Enlightenment, modifying the arguments as needed to take on new adversaries, such as Kant, Hegel, Darwin, and rationalist biblical critics. In the nineteenth century, a kind of literary warfare erupted between theologians and scientists on the one hand and between theologians and secular historians on the other. In their zeal to repel all adversaries, apologists sometimes became too defensive. They were overinclined to dismiss new scientific and historical theories as attacks on the faith. But as time went on, some of these theories won general assent, forcing apologetics into embarrassing retreats. It is a mistake to assume, as some did, that the human sciences have nothing worthwhile to contribute to our knowledge about the physical universe, human origins, and biblical history.

In the early twentieth century, the Protestant world especially in the United States became divided into two camps. Liberal theologians devised a new style of apologetics, which entered into dialogue with secular thought and took scientific investigation seriously. Trying to meet the adversaries on their own ground, they made concessions that were difficult to reconcile with traditional Christian faith. Trying to fit Christianity into the framework of a secular worldview, some depicted Jesus as a very good man, but scarcely the God of traditional orthodoxy. In reaction against such dilutions of the faith, fundamentalists stood for a literalist interpretation of Scripture that many educated Christians regarded as naive.

A third option, in addition to liberalism and fundamentalism, emerged in the form of neo-orthodoxy, under the leadership of the great Swiss Reformed theologian, Karl Barth. Unlike the liberals, Barth vigorously defended the central Christian dogmas such as the Trinity, the Incarnation, and the bodily resurrection of Jesus. He mounted a sustained attack on the liberalism of the previous century, discrediting Friedrich Schleiermacher and his disciples. The Christian dogmas, Barth insisted, should not be tailored to make them more acceptable to reason. The word of God, in his view, ought to be accepted in its fullness, even when it ran against all human expectations. It is of the very nature of faith to believe in hard sayings and astonishing events that humiliate our reason.

Barth, however, rejected the apologetical strategies of the fundamentalists. Reveling in paradoxes, he developed a subtle dialectical theology in which the word of God mysteriously came to us through human words, without requiring that these human words be free from error. In his view, the fundamentalists suffered from a rationalism of their own, because they overlooked the element of mystery in revelation. Faith, for Barth, is not the conclusion of a rational process but rather God's work in us. Apologetics, in his view, was the enemy of faith.

Toward the middle of the twentieth century, a number of Catholics came to agree with Barth on the perils of apologetics. Followers of the French Jesuit Pierre Rousselot reminded the apologists that faith is a sheer gift of God, a grace, enabling us to see what reason alone could not perceive. To believe is simply to accept the word of God, because it is his. The believer, like the lover, does not demand reasons. To ask why we should believe God's word is to show a lack of trust in God as witness. According to these theologians, we do not believe because we see the force of the evidence. On the contrary, we see the meaning and demonstrative value of the signs because we believe. For them understanding does not lead to faith, but faith is the source of understanding.

The schools of thought just considered provided three arguments against apologetics: First, the liberals objected that apologetics, as practiced by conservatives, is too defensive; that it resists the growth of understanding made possible through the advance of human sciences. Second, neo-orthodox Protestants objected that apologetics as practiced by liberals dilutes revelation in trying to make it acceptable to reason. Third, Catholic dogmaticians objected that conventional apologetics was too rationalistic; it failed to recognize that faith is a grace and cannot be produced by arguments.

As a result of charges such as these, apologetics acquired a bad reputation except in fundamentalist circles. Protestant theologians in the mainline churches were almost unanimous in claiming to be postapologetic or nonapologetic. In Catholic seminaries and universities the discipline of apologetics, which had been a major course in the theological curriculum until Vatican II, suddenly vanished. Its place was often taken by a new discipline known as fundamental theology, which dealt with Christian revelation and its transmission as seen in the light of faith.

But in this respect, as in so many others, fashions change. A great reawakening of apologetics has been taking place, led by Protestant Evangelicals here in the United States. Conservative Reformed and Baptist theologians, moving away from the fundamentalism of their fathers, have sought to find a new harmony between faith and reason, resurrecting the discipline of philosophy, which in Evangelical circles had fallen on hard times. Their new emphasis on Christian philosophy and apologetics has proved very effective in producing ardent believers eager to spread the gospel message.

Catholics, it would seem, are gaining a new appreciation of the importance of apologetics. In this country we already have a small army of new apologists, many of them—but by no means all—converts from Evangelical Protestantism. Authors such as Peter Kreeft, Karl Keating, Scott and Kimberly Hahn, Dale Vree, Thomas Howard, Patrick Madrid, and the late Sheldon Vanauken are prominent figures in this movement. Not satisfied to imitate contemporary biblicist Protestantism, the new Catholics are looking back a century or so and retrieving the insights of brilliant literary converts such as Cardinal Newman and G. K. Chesterton. Contemporary Catholic apologists also draw heavily on the work of some theologically orthodox Anglicans such as C. S. Lewis.

Uses of Apologetics

What are the uses of apologetics? In defending it, we should beware of exaggeration. First, we should recognize that apologetics is not absolutely necessary for authentic faith. If it were, faith would not be possible for anyone who had not studied apologetics. But we know well that there are many children and uneducated persons who have a strong faith without ever having read a word of apologetics. Even educated Christians, I suspect, frequently believe because the faith was instilled in them at an early age, and they have never found any good reason to doubt its truth.

Second, apologetics is not sufficient. If anyone were to accept Christianity simply on the basis of rational demonstrations, that person would not be making an act of Christian faith. Faith is a submission to the word of God, motivated by the authority of God who reveals and invites us to assent by implanting an inclination to believe in our hearts. An excessive reliance on apologetics can sometimes blunt a person's readiness to embrace the great mysteries of revelation.

Apologetics has a more modest task. It seeks to show why it is reasonable, with the help of grace, to submit to the word of God as it comes to us through Scripture and the Church. Faith is a free human act, and as such it has to be in accordance with reason. Believers may of course have all sorts of unsolved difficulties against faith. But if they are convinced that there can be no good answer to the objections and that faith is unreasonable, they cannot assent to revealed truth, or at least they cannot assent in a peaceful and untroubled way.

Catholics like myself believe that nature and reason are essentially good, even through they can be misused. God does not want us to throw away reason, because he has constituted us as rational beings. Because we are human, we are obliged by our very nature to act according to the norm of right reason. The Catholic Church has taught, and continues to teach, that there are sufficient signs, so that as a result the assent of faith is objectively justifiable. The task of apologetics is to discover these signs and organize them in such a way that they are persuasive to particular persons.

The importance of apologetics is most evident in the case of converts. I can hardly imagine any adult coming to Christian or Catholic faith without having deliberated for some time and having found good reasons for adopting the faith. (Certainly I myself found reasons.) Before professing the creed potential believers ask themselves why they ought to believe that Jesus Christ was the incarnate Son of God, that he died for our salvation, and that he rose from the dead to lead us into everlasting life. They may or may not feel an emotional attraction to the Church, but such an attraction would not be a sufficient warrant for embracing the faith. Before people act on their feelings, they have to be able to assure themselves that the Christian message is not just a myth or an illusion. Apologetics serves to overcome the doubts of inquirers who are preparing to embrace the Christian faith.

Even cradle Catholics may experience crises of conscience in which they reach out for rational supports. Without the help of apologetics they may find themselves tormented by temptations that imperil their faith.

Educated Christians, as they move from childhood to adulthood, have to take personal responsibility for their faith. The more reflective they are, the more will they want to assure themselves that their faith is not contrary to the assured results of the various human sciences. If they negotiate this crisis successfully, they emerge with a solid faith capable of meeting serious objections. While the arguments can never prove the truth of Christianity, they can show that it is reasonable to believe and that the arguments against faith are not cogent or convincing. God's grace will do the rest.

Models of Apologetics

In the contemporary literature, we find many different styles or "models" of apologetics. Such variety is to be expected because the objections today come from so many different quarters. Apologetics has always adapted itself to the intellectual climate of the day. I should like to summarize seven approaches that are prominent in the current literature.

1. Classical apologetics. A tripartite form of apologetics became standard from the seventeenth century until the middle of the twentieth; it still survives in many important authors. The first step is to prove the existence of God and to show that God is able to reveal truths that human beings need to know in order to escape from ignorance and guilt and to prepare themselves for eternal life. The second step shows that God has in fact revealed himself as our Redeemer through the history of ancient Israel and especially through Jesus Christ. The third step, in Catholic manuals and treatises, shows that the Catholic Church is the authorized bearer of revelation, and that her teaching and ministry should therefore be accepted. Protestants sometimes omit the third step or alter it in order to demonstrate that their own form of Christianity is more faithful to Holy Scripture.

There is nothing really wrong with this tripartite method. It sustained itself for several centuries and still has power to convince large numbers of patient students. But many inquirers today do not have the philosophical aptitude or inclination required for the first stage of the argument. It is not surprising, therefore, that contemporary apologists usually prefer methods more accessible to the ordinary reader of our day.

2. Biblical evidentialism is very popular today both among Catholics and among Evangelicals. Proponents of this method do not usually reject the validity of the classical approach, but they contend that it is not necessary to engage in an abstract discussion of natural theology before attending to the historical facts. The objective evidence provided by the historical record, they hold, enables us to bypass the philosophical preambles. The miracles of Jesus and his resurrection, together with his claims of divinity, his sublime teaching, and his wonderful purity of life, surpass all our

expectations and give grounds for believing that Jesus is the incarnate Son of God, as claimed by the New Testament and Christian orthodoxy. Some evidentialists consider that the Shroud of Turin gives striking confirmation to the Gospel accounts of the passion and resurrection.

The evidential approach differs from the classical because it does not argue from the existence of God to the authenticity of the historical signs, but on the contrary, establishes the reality of God because God is the only reasonable explanation of signs, especially the great sign of the crucified and risen Jesus. If we believe in Jesus, we cannot fail to believe in the God whom Jesus proclaimed. It is possible to believe in God because he has revealed himself in history.

3. Another line of approach is to argue from the religious experience of believers, which is a kind of subjective evidence. Feeling interiorly drawn toward Christian faith, many inquirers practice something like a discernment of spirits. They sense that the inclination to believe comes not from any unworthy or selfish motive but from on high. The more they accede to this inclination, the more they find their minds filled with insights and their souls flooded with peace and spiritual joy. Because they find faith a happy dwelling place of the mind, they consider it prudent for them to believe.

As believers, they speak for themselves alone, but they know well from the testimonies of fellow believers that their experiences are not peculiar to themselves. The reported experiences of others confirm their analysis of their own religious experience. In their apologetics, they seek to convince nonbelievers to pay attention to the attractions of grace in their own lives.

4. Similar to this argument from experience is the traditional Augustinian argument from the yearning of the human heart. Human nature, according to this school, has within itself a void that God alone can fill. Tertullian wrote in the second century that the soul is naturally Christian. St. Augustine in his *Confessions* penned the famous sentence: "You have made us for yourself, O Lord, and our hearts cannot find rest until they rest in you." If we look within ourselves, these apologists declare, we find in our hearts an unquenchable desire to love, to serve, and to adore. We

are in search of an object that is worthy of our full adoration and obedience, one worthy of every sacrifice. That object we find revealed in the God of Jesus Christ. In finding the reality we latch onto it with delight. The act of faith, corresponding to the "eureka" of Archimedes, is a cry of joy.

5. Still another approach is the theological aesthetics of the late Swiss Catholic theologian Hans Urs von Balthasar. He begins not with the religious inquirer but, like evidentialists, with the object. But he does not look for signs of power such as the miracles and resurrection of Jesus. The most convincing sign for him is the beauty of God reflected in the figure of Jesus Christ, who totally surrenders himself on the cross for the sake of our redemption. The content of Christian revelation, for Balthasar, is its own evidence; it does not need to be supported by external signs and arguments. The light of faith is not something subjectively inhering in our own consciousness. Primarily, it is the luminosity of the sacred reality in which we believe. In opening our minds to that light, we become flooded with its radiance.

6. Another school is called "presuppositionalist." Identified with Cornelius Van Til, Carl Henry, and Francis Schaeffer, this approach appeals to Protestants who are deeply conscious of original sin. Our reason, they hold, is so corrupted by the Fall that it is incapable of establishing the truth of the Christian faith. But when we hear the gospel proclaimed, we can let it take hold of us and see what follows when we hold it to be true. The more we contemplate reality from the perspective of faith, the more intelligibility we find in the world of experience.

Conservative Protestants who use this argument generally begin with the presupposition that the whole of Scripture, as the word of God, is inerrant and infallible. Catholics, however, find that this is a rather large order to accept without evidence, even hypothetically. But Catholics sometimes use a similar method, beginning with the basic Christian doctrines. St. Anselm, one of the great medieval apologists, coined the formula, "faith seeking understanding." Believing, he said, enabled him to understand. In the twentieth century, Rousselot and his followers, mentioned above, revived this vision. Vatican II suggests this line of argument in the *Pastoral Constitution on the Church in the Modern World.*

After speaking of the mystery of the human person in the light of Christian revelation, it concludes: "Through Christ and in Christ the riddles of sorrow and death grow meaningful" (*GS* 22). Those who adhere to revelation in faith find that life becomes more meaningful and livable. They do not escape suffering, but they find ways of coping with suffering.

Apologetics, for followers of this school, presupposes faith. It is not a means of arriving at faith but a means of confirming and solidifying faith and responding to objections that could weaken faith.

7. Still another set of apologists, the last in my enumeration, argue from the patterns of history. Christ, for them, is the summit of human and cosmic history and the key to its interpretation. They are impressed by the way in which monotheism arose in ancient Israel, by the fulfillment of the messianic types and prophecies in the person of Jesus, and by the wonderful spread of the gospel in the early centuries, resulting in the conversion of the Roman empire. They hold that under the aegis of faith, civilization rose to new heights. Philosophy and the arts flourished as never before. Some are drawn by the wisdom of great thinkers such as Augustine and Aquinas. Others look at the history of art and literature. They admire the faith that inspired Dante, Fra Angelico, the composers of Gregorian chant, and the architects of the medieval cathedrals. They sense that Christianity, where it is accepted, sustains a magnificent culture, and that where Christ is rejected, culture declines. In the light of Christ, human history has a meaning, pointing forward to the full realization of the kingdom of God when Christ returns in glory. Christianity brought with it the idea that history has a meaning, a purpose, and a goal.

Concluding Thoughts

In my judgment, these seven approaches are all valuable, though each individual will have his or her own preferences. I do not find it necessary to choose among them. Many theologians today, including myself, prefer a convergent use of the signs and evidences. The combination of all the arguments is more impressive that any one of them taken alone.

As Newman pointed out in the mid–nineteenth century, signs that are weak in themselves can become strong when confirmed by other signs pointing in the same direction. The convergence of the signs is a new fact requiring to be explained. A report of one individual about a miraculous event is usually not convincing, but if it is confirmed by dozens of other reports that independently corroborate it, it may become credible.

Signs that are mutually confirmatory may be considered in any order. There is no need to begin with the existence of God, and then pass through the fact of revelation to the authority of the Church. One may begin at any point in the circle. One can find Christ and the Church through God, or find God and the Church through Christ, or find God and Christ through the Church.

The logic of discovery is different from that of syllogistic deduction. There is no set of objective rules that can be mechanically applied to tell us when the evidence is sufficient to make out the case. The ultimate decision is a matter of prudence or good judgment—an exercise of what Newman called the "illative sense."

In the case of revealed religion, special attention must be given to the testimony of witnesses. The New Testament writers speak of the empty tomb and the resurrection with such conviction that we cannot doubt that the early Christians were sincerely convinced of these facts on the strength of eyewitnesses.

In its full dimensions, the religious testimony of committed witnesses is of a different character than that of witnesses in court or witnesses to ordinary historical events. Witnesses to the faith are consciously testifying to the transcendent, by which they are grasped. This kind of testimony is mysterious in its power. Witnesses sent by God into the world are like the prophets of old. They induce faith because they speak with a certain authority, analogous to that which the hearers of Jesus found in his words. Although, like Paul, they may lack eloquence, they glow with the fire ignited by the love of Christ, who speaks in and through them. They are living signs, personally transformed by the God whose grace is at work in them. The love of God communicates itself through his messengers, who are urged on by that love. As Balthasar said, "Only Love is credible."

In my own writings on apologetics, I have emphasized the category of testimony. Human relationships provide analogies. Belief ordinarily rests not on proof but on a relationship of trust. When there is such a relationship between a husband and a wife, they can count on one another to be faithful. For assurance of the other's fidelity, they do not need to exact an account of every moment of periods when they were separated. Within the Church we have an analogous network of relationships. God speaks to us through Jesus Christ, who speaks to us through those who wrote the Scriptures and through those who teach in his name in the Church. Faith is an interpersonal relationship with those who speak in the name of God. If we open ourselves to their testimony, we are able to enter into the new world of faith, which would otherwise remain inaccessible to us. Far from restricting us, faith extends the range of our experience and knowledge.

Apologists of a positivist mentality tried to prove the truth of the Gospels by the probing methods of critical scholarship. But in so doing they misunderstood the literary genre of the Gospels, which are written not as academic works of history but as testimonies of faith. The Gospels and other New Testament writings radiate the joy of the believing community and appeal to the reader to join the Church in her devout confession. If we read the Scriptures in that light, they confront us with the person of Jesus, who bears witness to his heavenly Father. It becomes possible for us to enter into the apostolic community of faith and to be sharers in its joy. The alternative is to resign ourselves to life without communion with the divine.

There are, of course, some norms for credible testimony. We cannot directly prove the content of the Christian message, but we can assess the credibility of the witnesses. We can show that the apostolic community was in a position to know the message and character of Jesus and the facts surrounding his life. We can show, in addition, that the first witnesses would not have tried to deceive their hearers. What motive would they have for such deception, when the proclamation of the faith was likely to lead to persecution and even martyrdom?

Apologetics is not designed to prove revelation beyond all possible doubt. If a person stands with folded arms and defiantly demands: "Prove it to me," he will never be satisfied. And even if the truth could be proved to him, it would not benefit him. Faith has to be free, not coerced; loving, not reluctant. What apologetics can do is to show that the act of faith is something that a person might reasonably perform, much as we believe the testimony of a beloved friend or mentor. This demonstration is not absolutely necessary, because it is possible to believe without ever having studied apologetics. Nor is it sufficient, because faith is a gift of God. But it is useful because it clears away obstacles and prevents us from suspecting that our faith is foolish and groundless. Apologetical arguments have often brought unbelievers to the point where they could seriously consider the claims of Christian faith, and in many cases have resulted in conversion. Out of love for potential converts, believing Christians seek to show that their faith is reasonable. They themselves strive to become credible witnesses.

Apologetics has to be tailored to each culture and in a sense to each individual. We all believe on motives personal to ourselves. The most convincing manual of apologetics, for most of us, is one that we write for ourselves. I invite you, my reader, to try to write down, at your leisure, the reasons why you might become, or are, and continue to be, a Christian believer, a Catholic, or whatever religion you profess.

Sources

1. Evangelization: New Testament through Vatican II

Based on the lecture, "Vatican II and Evangelization," delivered at Loyola Marymount University, Los Angeles, California, December 17, 2005. Published in *The New Evangelization: Overcoming the Obstacles*, edited by Steven Boguslawski and Ralph Martin (Mahwah, NJ: Paulist Press, 2008), 1–12.

2. Paul VI and Evangelization

Based on the lecture "The Reception of *Evangelii Nuntiandi* in the West," delivered at the Istituto Paolo VI, Brescia, Italy, September 24, 1995. Published in *Pubblicazioni Dell'Istituto Paolo VI* 19 (1998): 244–50.

3. The Program: Paul VI, John Paul II, and the New Evangelization

Based on the lecture, "John Paul II and Evangelization," delivered at the John Paul II Symposium, Mundelein Seminary, October 21, 1998. Published under the title "John Paul II and the New Evangelization," in *Studia Missionalia* 48 (1999): 165–80.

4. The Gospel: Point of Contention and Convergence

A new piece incorporating elements from "Evangelization: The Self-Communication of the Gospel," given at Notre Dame Seminary, New Orleans, March 3, 1993, and "The Basic Christian Message as a Form of Ecumenism," given for the St. Paul's Institute of Evangelical Catholic Ministry, Madison, Wisconsin, April 2, 2005.

5. *Evangelization and Ecumenism*

Lecture, "Evangelization and Ecumenism," delivered at Education Parish Service's 25th Anniversary Symposium, Washington, DC, October 25, 2003. Published in *Origins* 33 (November 13, 2003): 399–401.

6. *The Evangelization of Culture and the Catholic University*

Lecture delivered at The Catholic University of America, Washington, DC, March 16, 2004. Published in *Journal of Law, Philosophy and Culture* 1 (Spring 2007): 1–11.

7. *The New Evangelization and Theological Renewal*

Lecture delivered at Sacred Heart University, Fairfield, Connecticut, July 18, 1995. Published under the title "Evangelizing Theology," *First Things* No. 61 (March 1996): 27–32.

8. *Models of Evangelization*

Lecture delivered at St. Paul's Institute of Evangelical Catholic Ministry, Madison, Wisconsin, April 14, 2007. Published in *Origins* 37 (May 17, 2007): 8–12.

9. *Models of Catechesis*

Lecture prepared for Lansing, Michigan, Catechetical Day, October 20, 2007. Published under the title "Historical Models of Catechesis," *Origins* 37 (November 8, 2007): 347–52.

10. *Models of Apologetics*

Lecture, "The Changing Shape of Apologetics," delivered at the University of Missouri at Columbia, Missouri, February 10, 2006. Previously unpublished.